Program Your Microcomputer in BASIC

Of related interest

Beginning BASIC P. E. Gosling

Continuing BASIC P. E. Gosling

Microprocessors and Microcomputers Eric Huggins

Program Your Microcomputer in BASIC

P. E. Gosling, B.Sc., A.F.I.M.A.,
Principal Lecturer in Mathematics and Computing,
Peterborough Technical College

M

First published 1981 by
THE MACMILLAN PRESS LTD
London and Basingstoke

Companies and representatives throughout the world

ISBN 0 333 28654 5

Typeset in 10/12 IBM Press Roman by
Illustrated Arts, Sutton, Surrey
and printed in Hong Kong

Contents

Preface

This book is intended to introduce the BASIC language as offered on many microcomputers to the evergrowing number of people who have access to microcomputer systems. The reader is led through the use of elementary BASIC instructions by a series of carefully selected examples, and by a series of activities, each of which deals with a single instruction, or group of instructions. No previous knowledge of computing is needed, and such computing concepts as are necessary for the understanding of the text are explained as they arise.

To use this book, as Mrs Beeton almost said, 'First get your microcomputer'. Then read as much of the manufacturer's manuals and handbooks as you can follow, which probably will be just enough to get your computer working. Manuals tend to start easy but get obscure very quickly. This is where this book comes in. Once you have read the first twenty-four pages you should be ready to start on the activities. These activities are designed to be carried out in conjunction with the manufacturer's manual. No two versions of BASIC are identical so the activities should help you to understand the manuals better and just what your particular version of BASIC allows you to do.

Activity 15 is the most difficult, but potentially the most useful, feature of your computer; always assuming that it has some sort of backing store. With backing store you can save and retrieve information at will.

Take the activities slowly and make sure you understand each example. When in doubt, return to the manufacturer's manual. When you have successfully completed the activities you are on your own and should be able to write useful and exciting programs.

The author is very grateful to his many friends in the worlds of computing and education. They have all provided a great deal of help during the production of this book. In particular must be mentioned Roy Jones, Principal of Stamford College for Further Education, for the use of the college's 380Z, the Vice-Principal of Peterborough Technical College for the use of the college's CBM 3016 and Brian Duckworth, Head of Electrical Engineering at Peterborough Technical College, for the use of his department's SWTP 6400. Last minute help from Pat Ingram of the Cambridge Computer Store was also greatly appreciated as were the suggestions for improvements from Merl K. Miller.

Thanks are extended to Mike Osler of Newtons Laboratories, Douglas Benn of Health Computers Ltd. and Peter Walker of Stukely Computer Services for supplying programs which ran on their machines.

Photographs are reproduced by permission of IBM(UK) Ltd., Data General Ltd., Zygal Dynamics Ltd., Memec Systems Ltd., Research Machines Ltd. and Newtons Laboratories. Finally, many thanks to my son Patrick, for performing additional photographic work in between his school work and essential motor cycle maintenance.

P. E. Gosling

Introduction

In the past thirty years the influence of computers on our lives has grown dramatically so that there now seems to be no area of man's activity which is not affected by their use. This rapid infiltration into everyday life has been accompanied by a fall in the price of computer systems, so that now the 'home-computer' market seems to be rivalling the hi-fi market. Not many years ago a computer needed to be physically very large and required a special environment to sustain it. Not only that, but computing remained a mystery to the general public and highly-trained, specialised personnel were required to oversee the working of the machines. Due to the rapid advance of technology over the past ten years computers now fall into three main groups. The very large computers are still with us and are referred to as *mainframe* machines. Such computer installations, an example of which is shown in figure 1, still require special operating environments and large numbers of people to operate them. They are used mainly by the banks, large industrial concerns and the universities. The late 1960s saw the advent of the *minicomputer*, and because these machines

Figure 1 A large mainframe computer installation (*Photograph by courtesy of IBM United Kingdom Ltd*)

were exceptionally rugged and capable of working in quite primitive conditions, they soon found their way into aircraft, oilrigs, schools, small businesses, and even on to the backs of trucks and tractors. A typical minicomputer installation is shown in figure 2.

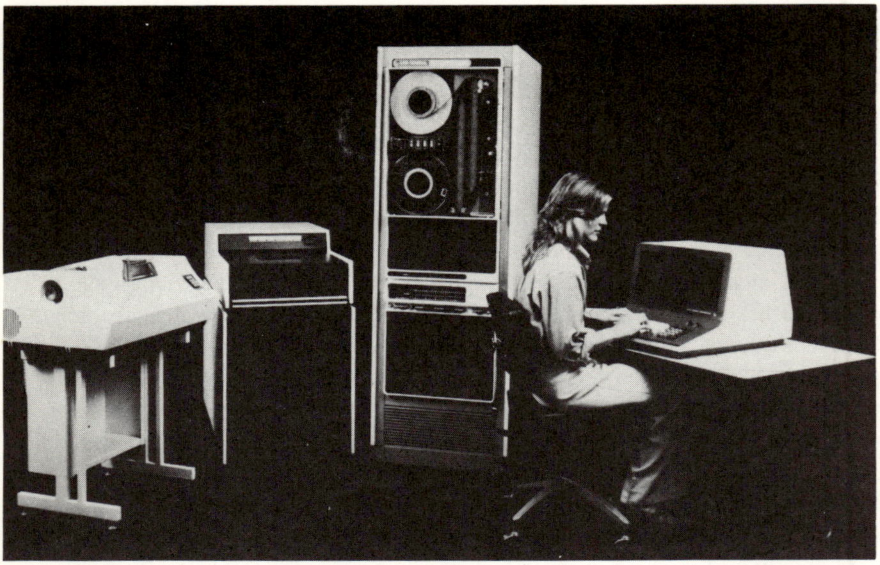

Figure 2 A typical minicomputer system (*Photograph by courtesy of Data General Ltd*)

The 1970s saw the development of the large-scale integrated circuit now referred to as the silicon chip. The technology of the chip makes it possible to compress very complex electronic circuits on to a tiny sliver of silicon no larger than one quarter of an inch square. Figure 3 gives some idea of the comparison between a minicomputer circuit board measuring 15 inches square, and the equivalent silicon chip encapsulated and ready to plug into a microcomputer circuit board.

The heart, or rather the 'brain', of a microcomputer is called its Central Processing Unit, the *microprocessor*, and this is central to all microcomputer systems. Not only has the silicon chip technology been used to compress the CPU into a very small area but the bulky memories used by the earlier generations of computers have also been miniaturised. Figure 4 shows an enlargement of a core memory plane from a mainframe computer of the 1960s – the wires were usually threaded by hand! Compare that picture with a modern silicon chip memory, as shown in figure 5, resting on a fountain pen nib. At present (1980) silicon chips are coming on to the market with the capability of storing approximately 64 000 bits of computer information. A bit (see the glossary) is a binary digit and is the basic unit of computer information used by

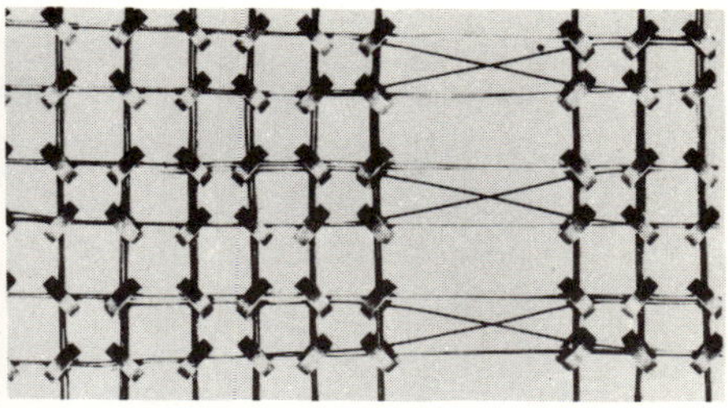

Figure 4 Close-up of core memory (*Photograph by courtesy of IBM United Kingdom Ltd*)

Figure 3 Minicomputer central processor circuit board and its micro-processor equivalent (*Photograph by courtesy of Data General Ltd*

all computers. The chip shown in figure 5 is such a chip. Each of the ferrite rings on the memory shown in figure 4 is capable of storing one bit only.

By linking up the microprocessor and the equally tiny memories we have the beginnings of a microcomputer. A number of different microcomputer systems are shown in figure 6.

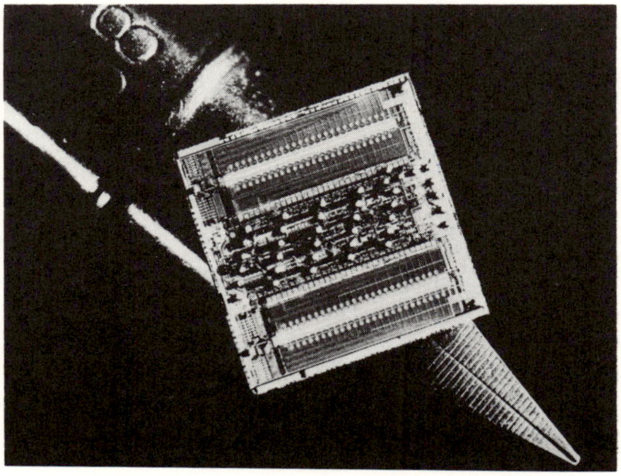

Figure 5 64K bit memory chip compared with a fountain pen nib (*Photograph by courtesy of IBM United Kingdom Ltd*)

Figure 6 **(a) Microcomputer system with twin floppy disc drives, keyboard and video screen (*Photograph by courtesy of Stukely Computer Services*)**

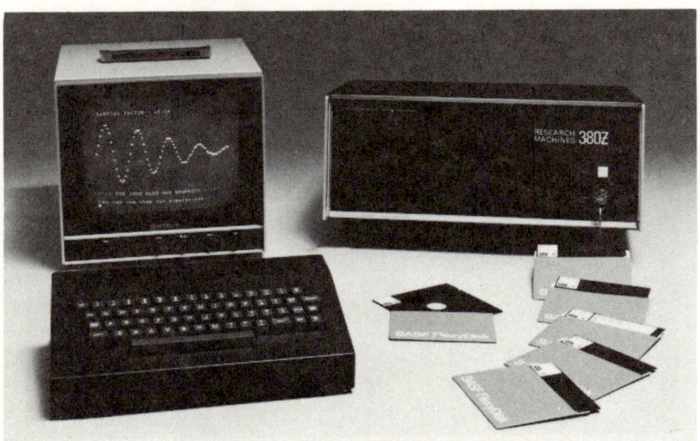

(b) microcomputer system with 5¼ inch floppy discs (*Photograph by courtesy of Research Machines Ltd*)

(c) microcomputer system with twin floppy disc drives and printer
(*Photograph by courtesy of Zygal Dynamics Ltd*)

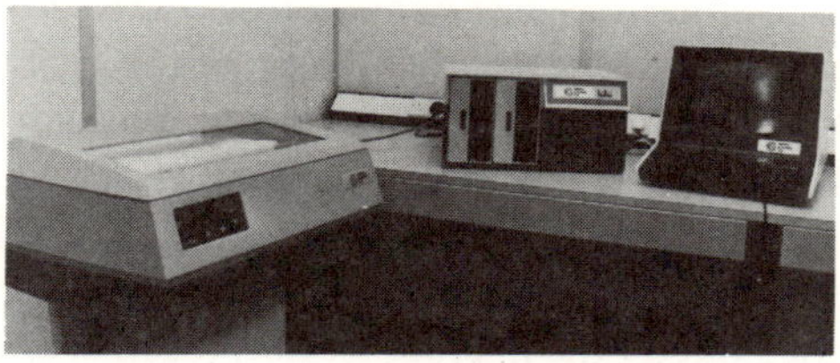

(d) microcomputer system with twin floppy discs and printer
(*Photograph by courtesy of Memec Systems Ltd*)

(e) microcomputer system with cassette storage and printer
(*Photograph by courtesy of Memec Systems Ltd*)

There are signs that microprocessors and memories will become even smaller during the next few years and this will mean that microcomputers will become more and more powerful. There is not much chance, however, that the actual size of computer systems will become much less. The size of people, in the long run, will stay the same and so the sizes of keyboards, television screens and printers will therefore also stay constant. The power and versatility of the microcomputer will go on increasing as the years pass. At the same time, it is quite certain that the cost of computing will come down, and so make more and more computing power available to more and more people, and to smaller and smaller businesses.

Without going into great detail let us consider the general layout of a microcomputer. It has already been pointed out that the microprocessor is central to the whole system. The microprocessor performs the arithmetic calculations and directs the results of these calculations to the various parts of the computer. The simplest form of microcomputer has no peripheral units except a keyboard and a video display, the latter often a domestic television set. Such a system is shown in figure 7. Even the simplest system must, however, have some way of storing the coded instructions which make the machine perform its arithmetic operations. In other words, the computer must have a memory. Computer memory is available in either very fast *immediate access store* or slower *backing store*. All computers need immediate access store, of the type shown in figure 5, while backing store is an optional, but very useful, addition to memory, as will be seen later. Backing store is in the form of either magnetic discs or magnetic tape. Immediate access store is usually referred to as RAM (Random Access Memory) and is the memory which stores the computer instructions currently being carried out by the microprocessor, together with the results of any calculations the microprocessor may have made.

Figure 7 A basic microcomputer

In addition to RAM, microcomputers have another form of fast memory called ROM (Read Only Memory). A ROM is a solid-state device, looking from the outside like any other integrated circuit, which contains certain instructions, essential to the working of the computer, permanently stored in it. These instructions cannot be modified in the same way that instructions stored in a RAM can be altered. A ROM is composed of physical links between bipolar devices which can only be altered by the destruction of some links and the insertion of others – a technique known as 'blowing a ROM'.

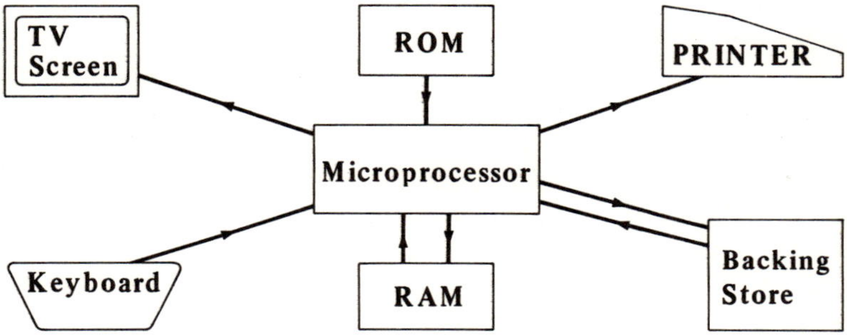

Figure 8 Block diagram of the main parts of a microcomputer system

A block diagram showing the main parts of a microcomputer system is shown in figure 8. Note the directions of the arrows which show the directions in which data can flow inside the machine.

The language used to communicate with most microcomputers is called BASIC (Beginner's All-purpose Symbolic Instruction Code). Instructions entered in BASIC at the keyboard have first of all to be converted into instructions which are immediately recognisable by the microprocessor. The machine code is a purely numeric code and is used internally by the computer, and the instructions for the conversion to machine code from BASIC are stored in RAM, having been read into this memory from some static memory device such as a ROM, magnetic disc or magnetic tape. RAM comes in various sizes, and the larger the amount of RAM a computer has the larger and more complex the programs it can handle. The very simplest microcomputer system will have its BASIC interpreter stored in ROM, and such a system is shown in figure 7. Such a system is very cheap but has a drawback in that it has no backing store. This means that every time a program is required to be run, all the instructions must be typed in at the keyboard. This is because anything stored in RAM is lost once the electrical power has been switched off. In addition, RAM can only store the program instructions for the current program, and this severely restricts the power of a simple system such as the one shown in figure 7.

The cheapest form of backing store is that available on magnetic tape cassettes. Figure 9 shows such a system where the backing store is provided by two domestic audio cassettes. These are used to store not only the BASIC interpreter, if it is not on a ROM, but also any program developed on the computer

Figure 9 Microcomputer with cassettes as backing store

and required for future use. Programs stored on a cassette can be read directly into RAM and be ready to use without the bother of typing them in at the keyboard. Backing store is also essential if a business system is to be run, since if files of data are to be kept and updated by the computer, they have to be in a form which is easily read by the computer.

Figure 10 shows backing store in the form of magnetic discs. These are discs of thin, flexible plastic and are coated with a magnetic material. The usual names given to these discs are 'floppy' discs or 'flexy' discs. The large-sized discs are 8 inches in diameter and the smaller type are 5¼ inches in diameter. It is possible, on some microcomputer systems, to have what are called 'hard' discs.

Figure 10 Dual floppy disc drive with an 8 inch floppy disc. Each drive unit has a capacity of 315K bytes (*Photograph by courtesy of Data General Ltd*)

These are the type of discs usually attached to mini or mainframe computers and are very much larger than floppy discs and thus can store much more data. The particular advantage of discs over tape is that data can be written and retrieved very quickly, whereas the speed with which this can be done on cassette tapes is restricted by the speed of the tape moving past the magnetic reading/writing heads, that is, 1⅞ inches per second.

A complete microsystem consisting of disc drives, video screen and keyboard is shown in figure 11. A system with a hard disc drive is shown in figure 12. Such systems are fine for many purposes but have a serious drawback in that they have no facility for what is called *hard copy*, unless the screen is photographed! In other words, in order to complete a computer system, some form of printer is required. When a printer is connected, the system is then capable of producing invoices, letters, tabular information, name and address labels or even cheques. Special types of printers can be used in conjunction with a microcomputer system so that diagrams, music or working drawings for engineers, for example, could be produced.

Figure 11 A complete microcomputer system with two integral floppy disc drives, keyboard and video screen (*Photograph by courtesy of Zygal Dynamics Ltd*)

From the above discussion it can be seen that, according to configuration, a microsystem can be used for games, household accounting, office accounting, design work or even music scoring. These are only a few examples of the uses to which microcomputers can be put. The degree of complexity of the job which a system is required to do will determine the 'hardware' required.

Figure 12 Microcomputer system with backing store on a hard disc (*Photograph by courtesy of Newtons Laboratories*)

Review questions – Test your knowledge of computers large and small

1. Which of the following activities could be 'computerised'?
   (a) Designing a bridge
   (b) Writing a political speech
   (c) Judging a beauty contest
   (d) Writing a pop song
   (e) Designing a crossword puzzle
   (f) Predicting the economic growth of a country
   (g) Controlling the flow of traffic through a city
2. What are the essential differences between a mainframe computer, a minicomputers and a microcomputer?
3. If you had a microcomputer in your home what *useful* tasks could you give it?
4. 'Computers can produce the greatest invasion of privacy of all time'. Do you agree?
5. What obstacles are there in the way of producing a true pocket computer?

Conversing with a Computer

The usual way in which we converse with a computer is through a series of *program* instructions and *command* words. A program instruction is one which tells the computer to perform some operation on a number stored in RAM. These operations are, in general, of an arithmetic nature (add, subtract, multiply, divide), and a typical program instruction would be to retrieve two numbers from RAM, add them together, and return the answer to some specified location in RAM.

A command word, on the other hand, is an instruction to do something to a complete program or set of data, often called a file. For example, the command RUN will cause the program currently stored in RAM to be executed, one instruction at a time. Program instructions are generally written in BASIC, and these are loaded into RAM either from the keyboard or from backing store. Program instructions are stored in RAM in an order dictated by a *line number* which has to precede every instruction. When the command RUN is issued, the BASIC interpreter program is called into action. This is a special program which scans each line of BASIC. The first thing the interpreter does is to detect any errors there might be in each line of the program. If no errors are found then the program instructions are translated into machine code and executed by the microprocessor. BASIC acts as an interface between you, the user, and the microprocessor. BASIC, like any other language, has its rules and conventions. These have to be followed by us so that the machine can obey our instructions in exactly the way in which we want them to be obeyed.

A typical BASIC program to multiply two numbers together would consist of the following program instructions

```
1Ø INPUT X, Y
2Ø Z = X*Y      (Sometimes LET Z = X*Y is used, but this is going out of
3Ø PRINT Z        fashion)
4Ø END
```

Although the details of BASIC have not yet been covered the meaning of these instructions should be fairly simple to follow. The first line instructs the computer to accept two numbers from the keyboard and to place them in RAM at 'addresses' known as X and Y. The second line is an instruction to retrieve the two numbers previously stored in RAM, multiply them together and place the result of that multiplication into an address called Z. Note that we use * for the multiplication symbol. The third line of the program is an instruction to copy the contents of the location known as Z on to the video screen. The last line is the way we tell the computer that we have reached the end of our list of instructions. All lines in BASIC are numbered and there are very good reasons, as you will see later, for numbering the lines in steps of 10.

Although it would appear that the program referred to above is of a trivial nature it serves to illustrate some essential points. One of these is the ability of BASIC to detect errors caused by typing mistakes. It would not be difficult to type the program in as follows

```
1Ø IMPUT X,Y
2Ø LET Z = X:Y
3Ø PRIMPT Z
4O END
```

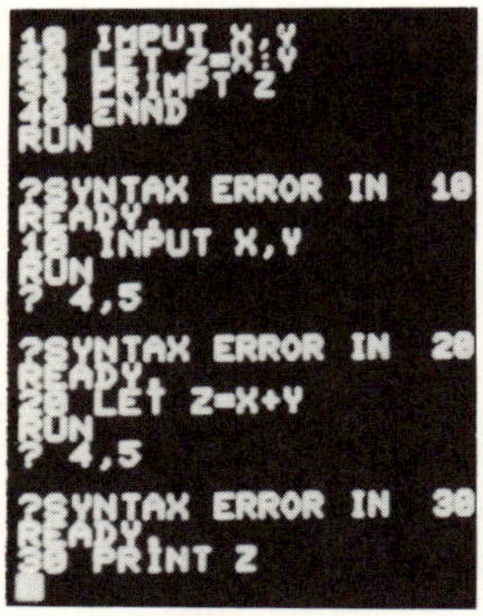

Figure 13 (a)

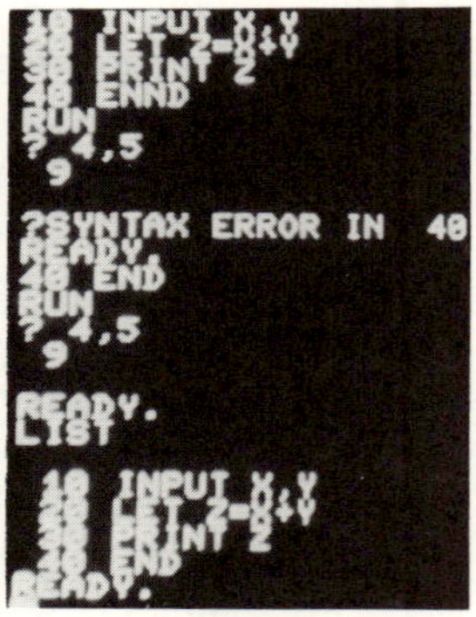

Figure 13 (b)

Figure 13 shows the effect of typing in the 'program' and attempting to run it. Note that only the current error is detected, so that all lines up to the line in error are executed. The program comes to a halt only when an error is detected in the BASIC instruction or when the last instruction has been reached.

Note also the general poor quality of the error messages, which is typical of most micro-systems. They will often indicate that an error exists at a particular line, but fail to identify the error in detail. The word *syntax* covers a multitude of sins! There are even times when an error is detected in a line where there is no apparent error. On the line being retyped the error mysteriously disappears. You have been warned!

Basic BASIC

A program is a series of logically arranged instructions, written in a language capable of being understood by the computer, whose object is to solve a particular problem. The program illustrated on page 11 solves the problem, 'what is the product of two numbers ?' The very simplest type of program is one which instructs the computer to perform arithmetic calculations. We shall see later that we have certain instructions available which will enable us to instruct the computer to make logical decisions. These take the computer far beyond the facilities of a mechanical calculating machine.

BASIC has three fundamental program instructions, referred to as types 1, 2 and 3. These are:

(1) Instructions which cause data to be loaded into RAM addresses.
(2) Instructions which cause the microprocessor to carry out an arithmetic operation on data stored in RAM.
(3) Instructions which cause data to be copied from an address in RAM and displayed on a suitable peripheral unit such as a video screen.

The simplest example of the first group, type 1, uses the BASIC word INPUT.

```
  1Ø INPUT X
   ↑        ↖
  line        open a channel from the keyboard to a location
 number       in RAM referred to as X
```

```
  1Ø INPUT X,Y
```

is an instruction to transfer two numbers from the keyboard to locations in RAM known as X and Y. The list following the word INPUT is known as the *input list*. Items in this list are separated by commas. The input list can be as long as you like, provided that the list can be contained on one line. In BASIC the letters of the alphabet are used to stand for *variables*. A variable is a number whose value is not known at the time the program is written. Its value will, of course, be assigned as soon as an INPUT instruction is executed. At that time a numerical value is assigned to the variable and it is this number which is stored in

RAM in a location referred to by that variable name. Variable names are sometimes known as *symbolic addresses*. In order to give a greater range of variable names than the twenty-six letters of the alphabet would allow, the name can consist of a letter followed by a single digit, 0 to 9. This means that names such as B1, C9 or FØ, for example, are legal BASIC. In some versions of the language the number of legal names is made even greater by extending the rules for naming variables. Two extensions are:

(1) Names can be represented by words, which can easily be recognised for what they are. Instead of T, for example, TOTAL can be used. In some versions of BASIC, however, only the first two characters of the name are significant. This would mean that MEAN and MEDIAN would both be stored in the same address in RAM. Consult the manufacturer's manual before using names with more than two characters.

(2) Names representing integers (whole numbers), as opposed to decimals with perhaps 6 or 8 significant digits, are denoted as such by a percentage sign after the name. A% would represent an integer number, whereas A would refer to a quite different number with as many as 8 significant digits.

BASIC recognises constants as well as variables, a constant being a number whose value remains unchanged throughout a program. Program instructions of type 2 will indicate that an arithmetic operation is to be performed on variables and constants by means of a statement such as

```
2Ø LET P = 4 + Q – (3/R) †
```

which is an instruction to divide the value of the variable called R into the constant 3. The result of this calculation is to be subtracted from the variable Q and that answer added to the constant 4. The result of the calculation is to be stored in RAM under the variable name P. The values of Q and R remain unaltered after this instruction has been executed. Only copies of the current values of variables are manipulated by the microprocessor. An instruction of the form

```
2Ø LET P = P + 4 †
```

will, of course, alter the value of P since the instruction tells the microprocessor to add 4 to the value of the variable P and then place the result in RAM in the address formerly occupied by the previous value of P. BASIC does all the allocating of addresses in RAM and so we do not need to know exactly where any of the variables and constants are located.

† Remember that the word LET is optional

There are five arithmetic operations in BASIC. These are

Operation	*Symbol*
Addition	+
Subtraction	–
Multiplication	*
Division	/
Exponentiation (raising a number to a power)	↑

LET is the BASIC instruction which causes a formula to be evaluated. There can be only one variable on the left hand side of the = sign. In fact, the = sign, when it follows a LET, is really an instruction and not a sign of equality. In this context = means 'take the value of'.

A few examples of formulae and their BASIC equivalents are shown below.

Formula	*BASIC instruction*
Volume = length x breadth x height	2Ø LET V = L*B*H
Area = ½base x height	2Ø LET A = Ø.5*B*H
Interest = principal x time x rate/100	2Ø LET I = P*T*R/1ØØ
Volume = $\frac{4}{3}\pi$ radius^3	2Ø LET V = 4/3*3.142*R↑3

When BASIC executes a LET instruction it does so according to a very strict set of rules. These state that any part of a formula enclosed within brackets is evaluated before anything else. When that has been done then any part of the formula containing the exponentiation sign has the next highest priority. Multiplication and division are the next in order to be executed. Finally addition and subtraction are performed. If a formula has nothing but operations of the same level of priority then it is evaluated from left to right. Thus the formula

$$\frac{a \times b}{c \times d}$$

will be written in BASIC as

```
A*B/C/D
```

or

```
(A*B)/C*D)
```

but not as

```
A*B/C*D
```

None of the operational symbols may be left out so that the operation of multiplying 6 by A must be written as

```
6*A
```

not

```
6A
```

The operation of multiplying the sum of A and B by 4 must be written as

```
4*(A + B)
```

not as

```
4(A + B)
```

The first of the activities which follow this section contains a practical example of the results of the sequence of the various arithmetic operations. Whenever there is any chance of ambiguity then it should be resolved by the liberal use of brackets.

Program instructions of type 3 will look like

```
3Ø PRINT Z
```

or

```
3Ø PRINT P,Q
```

where the word PRINT causes a channel to be opened, from the locations referred to in the list following this key-word, to the video screen.

The word END is usually placed at the physical end of a program. Not all versions of BASIC, however, will require this.

We now return to the progam listed on page 11, namely

```
1Ø INPUT X,Y
2Ø LET Z = X*Y
3Ø PRINT Z
4Ø END
```

Once this program has been typed in, and loaded into RAM, the command RUN, followed by depression of the RETURN key, can be issued. Remember that the RETURN key is your way of telling the computer to accept the line of program or the command you have just typed in. It will not take any action on

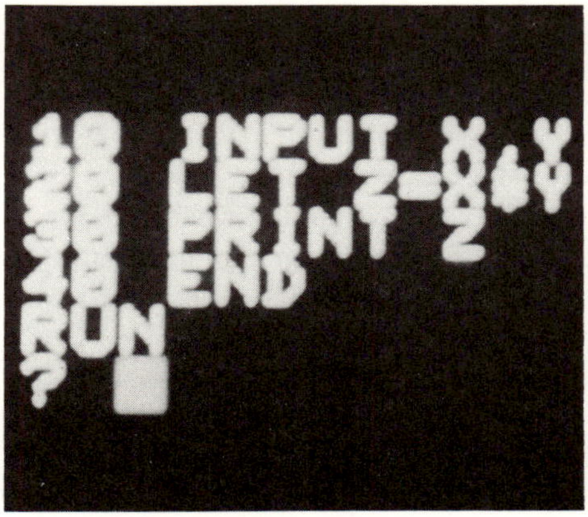

Figure 14

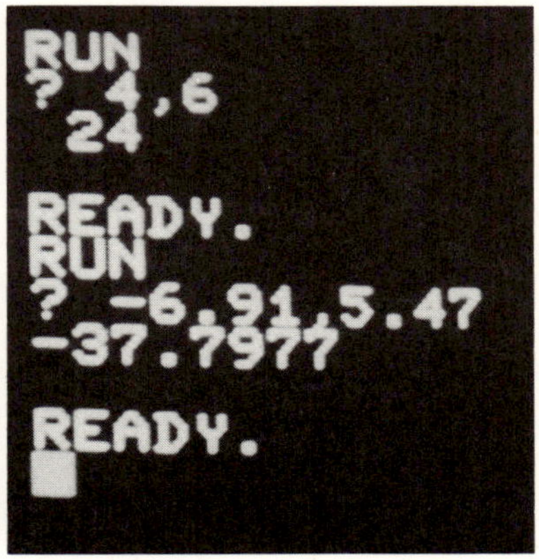

Figure 15

that line until you have pressed RETURN. In the same way the computer sends you a signal, called a *prompt*, in the form of an easily-recognisable character (* or : for example), which is its way of saying 'over to you'. The ? symbol used while a program is running is its prompt asking for some form of input into the program. Once the RUN instruction has been issued then the BASIC program is executed one statement at a time, starting with the one with the lowest line number. Figure 14 shows the result as displayed on the video screen. Notice that the first thing the program does is to issue the ? prompt which indicates that it has reached the INPUT instruction at line 10. Two items of data, corresponding to the variable names X and Y have to be typed in, separated by commas. Then the program will carry on and execute lines 20 and 30. Then it will stop. Figure 15 shows the result of running the program with two different sets of data.

Constants in BASIC can be typed into the computer in various forms, but different types of numbers are stored in different ways in RAM. For example, an *integer* (a whole number) is stored in RAM in a different way from a number containing a decimal point (a so-called *floating-point number*). The type of number is decided by the name you choose for it. If you have a version of BASIC which uses only integers, then all variable names refer to integers. This gives rise to some strange results if you are not prepared. For example, the result of dividing 8 by 3 in an integer BASIC will be stored as 2. If your version of BASIC allows you to state that some variables are to be integers then the variable name will be followed by a percentage sign (%). Otherwise all variables are stored as floating-point numbers. Whatever kind of numbers are used in your program they require a sign in front only if the number is negative. If no sign is typed, the number is assumed to be positive. No response made to a ? prompt may contain commas. This is because the comma is used to indicate when one number finishes and another begins. For example, if

```
55 INPUT X
```

is the current line being executed, then a response of

55,786

meaning fifty-five thousand, seven hundred and eighty-six, to the ?, is not capable of being understood by the computer. You have given it what it thinks are two numbers separated by a comma; it can allocate the first, 55 to X but it does not know what to do with the 786. As a result BASIC will issue an error message, and refuse to continue with the program.

Floating-point numbers can be input using the full stop on the keyboard as the decimal point. Very large, and very small, numbers can be input in a special way. This is the so-called *E format*, where the letter E stands for 'times 10 to the power of'. Instead of typing 1030000 we could type

1.03E6

which stands for

1.03×10^6

In the same way the number

0.00000678

could be input as

6.78E–6

standing for

6.78×10^{-6}

On input a + sign after the E is optional (1.006E6 is the same as 1.006E+6 or 1.006E+06) but BASIC always puts the appropriate sign in for you. A sign in front of the first digit applies that sign to the number as a whole. For example

–1.006E6 = -1.006×10^6

but

1.006E–6 = 1.006×10^{-6}

and

–1.006E–6 = -1.006×10^{-6}

When the computer displays numbers on the video screen it will always display very large, or very small, numbers in the E format. See figure 16.

Once the program has been run with one set of data it can be rerun using a totally different set of input data. Your program is stored in RAM until you make a decision to erase it. Computers are very single-minded and will execute only the one program stored in RAM at any one time.

Figure 16

A program in RAM can be amended simply by typing in a line whose number is between any pair of line numbers already in the program. BASIC will then slot your new line in between your existing lines at the appropriate point. A line already in your program can be changed if you type in a replacement line bearing the same number as that of the line you wish to replace. An unwanted line can be deleted by typing its line number alone. Figure 17 shows this at work. Note the effect of the LIST command which causes the current program to be listed on the video screen.

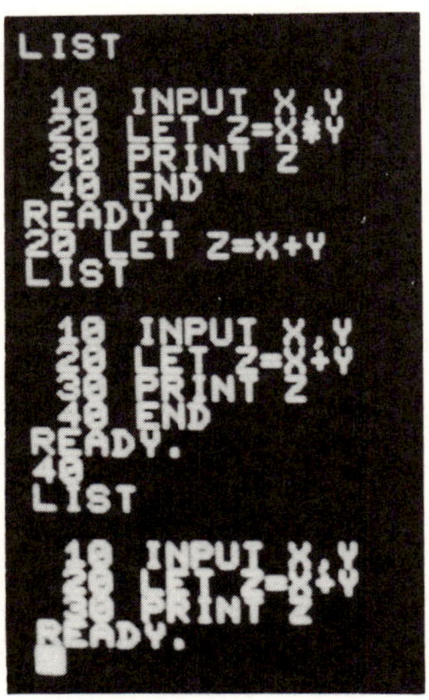

Figure 17

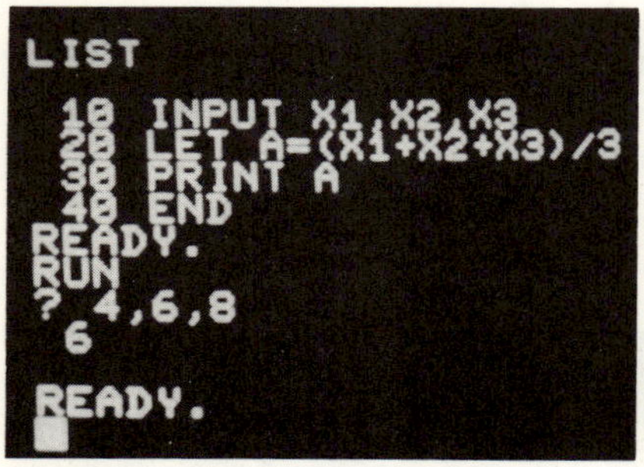

Figure 18

Figure 19

Figure 18 shows a program which calculates the average of three numbers. Figure 19 shows a program which calculates the volume of a sphere using the formula

$$v = \frac{4}{3}\pi r^3$$

Note that we have used the line

```
1Ø LET P = 3.14159
```

since there is no key for the Greek letter π on most microcomputer keyboards. In our example we have to assign the numerical value of π to the variable named P before the rest of the calculation takes place. Figure 20 shows a program which evaluates the formula

$$s = ut + \frac{1}{2}ft^2$$

for different values of u,t and f.

The final example in this section, figure 21, shows a program which evaluates the formula

$$x - (x^3/6) + (x^5/120)$$

which is called the *sine* function.

To gain practice and experience in writing programs in BASIC you should now complete the series of activities which follow. They are designed to give a graded approach to the art of writing programs. When typing in the programs which form the activities you will find that typing errors are easy to correct. There is no need for you to be a demon typist when using a computer; all you need is the *backspace* key, sometimes marked *delete* or *rub-out*. Each depression of this key will cause the cursor on the screen to move back one space. When the character you wish to change has been reached, you can continue typing the line from that point. Deletion and replacement of lines have already been dealt with a few paragraphs back.

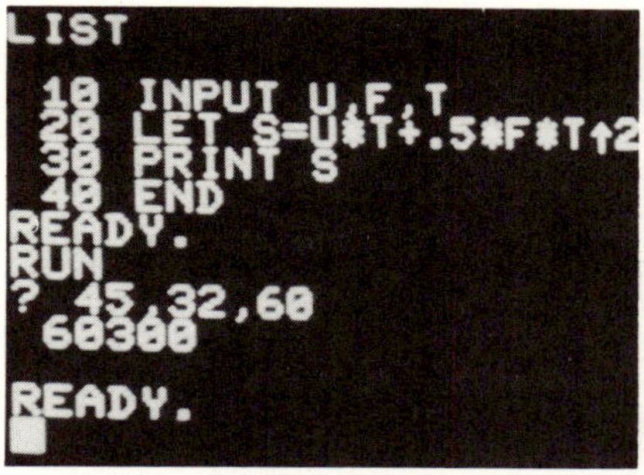

Figure 20

Figure 21

The activities have been designed so that they can be run using most versions of BASIC currently available. They should be carried out in conjunction with the manufacturer's handbook of BASIC supplied with your microcomputer. If the results expected from any program do not tally with what actually happens then you should consult the handbook. BASIC exists in a number of different dialects and every effort has been made in this book to produce a version of BASIC compatible with as many of the variants as possible. All the activities have been tried out on a series of microcomputers in an effort to eliminate most of the problems of compatibility. The largest area of difference lies in activity 15, file handling, where a large number of different systems have been used to run the same program but using statements peculiar to each version of BASIC.

If you have finished with a program, and wish to replace it in RAM with another, then you can clear the program from RAM by means of the NEW command. Once the NEW command has been typed in, a new program can be entered. If you do not type NEW then the new program will simply overlay the existing one, with disastrous results. BASIC will not recognise the statements as being those for another program. Even computers cannot read minds!

A program can be saved on disc or cassettes, if your system has these types of backing store, by means of the SAVE command. SAVEing a program will cause a copy of the program currently in RAM to be transferred to the backing store. You will still have to issue the NEW command if you want to enter a new program after saving the old one. A program saved on backing store can be brought into RAM by the LOAD command. If this is done then the system automatically executes a NEW before loading the progam from backing store into RAM. A program which is saved must be referred to by a unique name so that it can be catalogued by the operating system (q.v.). When a program is to be retrieved from backing store it must be referred to by its name. See figure 22.

You will notice that some of the programs in the activities contain REM statements. These are REMarks about the program. They form no part of the program, merely contain descriptive matter, and do not affect the running of the program in any way. Remember that REM statements are stored as a string of characters and these are very wasteful of memory space. Every character in the REM statement takes up one byte of memory – see page 24. There are a number

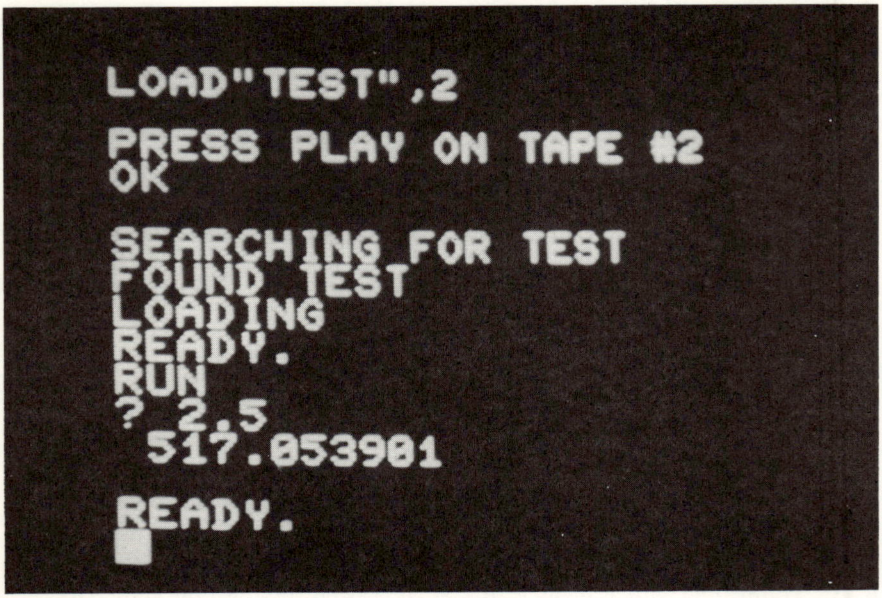

Figure 22

of ways of conserving the amount of memory taken up by a program. Usually the manufacturer's manual will tell you ways of saving space. A common one, for example, is to use the symbol ? instead of the word PRINT.

Review questions

Before you start the activities, see if you can answer the following.

1. Are these valid BASIC names for variables on your machine?

(a) A1	(b) TOTAL	(c) %B	(d) C%
(e) END$	(f) NO OF ITEMS	(g) G61	(h) NØ(4)
(f) AS$%	(j) 4C	(k) F99%	(l) NO(4)

2. Are the following acceptable BASIC instructions on your machine?

(a) LET P = Q + R		(b) K = A + –B
(c) A+B = F	(d) D = 4AB	(e) C = A(D + 4)
(f) J=K↑–1/3	(g) J=K↑(–1/3)	(h) X = X*X
(i) K=P↑Q↑R	(j) A%=P+Q	(k) P$ = L% + A
(l) D = A$ + D$		

Glossary of Terms

Address – a numbered location in RAM which will contain one byte of information.

ASCII – American Standard Code for Information Interchange. A binary code in which characters are represented by a fixed number of binary digits.

Assembler – a coded form of instructions containing both alphabetic and numeric symbols. Can be translated into machine code before execution by a computer.

BCD – Binary Coded Decimal. A method of storing numbers inside a computer's memory such that each decimal digit is represented by its binary equivalent. For example, 1 is represented by 0001, 2 by 0010, etc., so that the decimal number 27 is coded as 00100111.

Binary – a number system which uses only the digits 0 and 1.

Bit – a binary digit, a zero or 1. This is because computers depend on electronic switches which are either on (1) or off (0).

Byte – a set of eight bits.

Channel – the path along which data flows between one part of a computer and another.

CPU – Central Processing Unit. The microprocessor itself. The part of the computer which controls the operation of all the other parts.

Decimal – a number system which uses the digits 0, 1, 2, 3, 4, 5, 6, 7, 8, 9 only.

EPROM – Erasable Programmable Read Only Memory. A special form of ROM which can have the coded data erased from it by electronic means and new data substituted.

Firmware – programs which are used by the computer but which are available 'burned' into a ROM. The program is therefore 'plugged in' to the computer, rather than being typed in, or read from magnetic tape or disc as is the case with software.

Hardware – the nuts and bolts of a computer. Sometimes referred to as 'the bits you can kick'.

Hexadecimal – a number system which uses the digits 0, 1, 2, 3, 4, 5, 6, 7, 8, 9 and the characters A, B, C, D, E, F. A stands for 10, B for 11 and so on.

High level language – a computer language, such as BASIC, FORTRAN or COBOL, written in such a way that it is easily understood by the programmer. Has to undergo a translation process before providing the machine code which can be understood by the computer.

Interface – a device which enables one piece of equipment to 'talk' to another.

Kilo – a prefix denoting one thousand. Hence one kilobyte is approximately 1000 bytes. In fact 1K in computer terms is 1024 (2^{10}).

Machine code – a numeric coded form of instructions capable of being interpreted directly by the CPU.

Mega – a prefix denoting one million.

Microsecond – one millionth of a second. (10^{-6}).

Nanosecond – one thousand millionth of a second. (10^{-9}).

Nibble – half a byte, that is, four bits.

Octal – a number system which uses the digits 0, 1, 2, 3, 4, 5, 6, 7.

Peripheral – a device connected to a microprocessor. For example, disc drives, printers, graph plotters, paper tape readers, etc.

Port – a data channel capable of being connected to a computer peripheral.

Program – a logical sequence of instructions executed by a computer in order to solve a problem.

RAM – Random Access Memory. Memory module which can have coded information both written to it or read from it. It is called a Random Access Memory since any location within it can be accessed directly and very quickly.

ROM – Read Only Memory. Memory Module which has coded information permanently 'burned' into it. A form of Random Access Memory which can only have data read from it.

Software – the programs used by a computer.

VDU – Visual Display Unit. A television monitor usually attached to a keyboard similar to a typewriter keyboard. Displays whatever is typed in, together with whatever output is generated by the computer.

Word – a unit of computer information. In most microcomputers one word consists of eight bits. Some microcomputers and most minicomputers use a word containing 16 bits. Mainframe computers have a word length of 24 or 32 bits.

Some useful information

In a microcomputer with an eight-bit word

(1) A signed integer takes up 2 bytes.
(2) A decimal variable takes up 4 bytes.
(3) A decimal variable expressed in double precision takes up 8 bytes.
(4) A single character takes up 1 byte.
(5) A single 5¼ inch floppy disc can store up to 715 000 bytes.
(8) A single 8 inch floppy disc can store up to a megabyte.
(9) RAM usually comes in multiples of 8K bytes.

Activity 1

General

```
10 INPUT X,Y
20 LET Z=X+Y
30 PRINT Z
40 END
```

Activity 1.1

Type in the program shown in activity 1.1; do not forget to press RETURN or CARR RETURN at the end of every line. If you have made any obvious mistakes while typing a line, do not forget that you can edit the line by using the BACKSPACE key, sometimes marked ERASE.

Now type the command RUN, followed by RETURN. The computer should respond with the ? prompt. This means that it now waits for you to type in the two numbers which will correspond with the variables named X and Y. Remember to separate the numbers with a comma, since you need to indicate where one number ends and the next one begins. The next thing to happen is that the sum of the two numbers you have typed in will be displayed on the screen, this being the computed value of the variable called Z. If you type RUN again, the computer will ask for a further pair of numbers. Again the computer will compute their sum and print it. It might be a good idea to type in a number of pairs of numbers in various formats. Remember that the decimal point is the full stop key, and that you can use the E format for very large or very small numbers.

When you are satisfied with your first attempt at programming, change the program by typing in a new version of line 20. One change you could make is to replace line 20 with the line

```
2Ø LET Z = X*Y
```

so that the program will now compute and print the product of the two numbers instead of their sum. Note that there must be a distinction made between a zero and the letter O. They are much the same to the human eye but represent different codes to the computer. Therefore we usually make sure there is no ambiguity by putting a slash through the zero. In the same way we cannot use the 1 and the capital I indiscriminately.

By using different arithmetic operators you can amend line 20 in many ways. These signs are +, –, *, / and ↑ . Each time you change a line it is good practice to use the LIST command, to cause all the existing lines of a program to be listed on the screen. This enables you to check that any changes have been made correctly. If you are satisfied with the program then you can RUN it.

When you are testing these programs note that there is a maximum number of digits which the computer will display, however many you may have typed in after the ? prompt. The exact number of significant digits printed by your computer will be given in the manufacturer's handbook and is not consistent from one manufacturer to another.

Try to develop the habit of checking mentally the answer which the computer presents to you. If you get an answer which is unexpected then it is almost certainly due to a programming error and not to a computer error. The program shown in activity 1.2 is an example of this. Its object is to calculate the

```
10 INPUT A,B
20 LET C = A+B/2
30 PRINT C
40 END
```

Activity 1.2

average of a pair of numbers. Type it in and run it. Use the numbers 0 and 4 as input. Then run it with 6 and 4 as input. Which run gives the correct answer, and why? See if you can correct line 20, which is the one in error, by using brackets (and). Brackets may be used to make the interpretation of an arithmetic operation clear and unambiguous. When you have replaced line 20, list the program and check it. Then rerun it using the same input as before. Then check it out with a few more pairs of numbers to make quite sure that it always works. Only when you are sure of your program and understand why the first version was incorrect should you continue with any further examples. Activity 1.3 illustrates the use and effect of brackets in arithmetic calculations. Type it in, but do not forget NEW first of all, and run it with a variety of sets of input data.

```
10 INPUT A,B,C,D
20 LET X=A+B*C^2/D
30 PRINT X
40 LET X=((A+B)*C^2)/D
50 PRINT X
60 LET X=A+(B*C)^2/D
70 PRINT X
80 LET X=(A+B*C)^2/D
90 PRINT X
100 LET X=(((A+B)*C)^2)/D
110 PRINT X
120 END
```

Activity 1.3

Activity 2

Mathematical

```
10 INPUT X
20 LET Y=SQR(X)
30 PRINT Y
40 END
```

Activity 2.1

In order to simplify the way we write programs which perform arithmetic calculations, BASIC provides us with all the facilities we expect from a book of mathematical tables. The accuracy provided by the computer is far in excess of that provided by the tables. For example, the SQR function will provide us with the square root of a number and this is accomplished by writing

SQR(*var*)

where *var* is a variable name. Type in and run the program shown in activity 2.1. Whatever number you type in response to the ? prompt will have its square root calculated and printed. Try with a selection of numbers, large and small. See what happens if you type in a negative number.

In addition to the SQR function BASIC allows you to use a wide range of mathematical functions and the most common are

SIN(X)	sine of x
COS(X)	cosine of x
TAN(X)	tangent of x
ATN(X)	arc tan of x
LOG(X)	natural logarithm of x
EXP(X)	e^x

All the trigonometrical functions will require the value of x to be in radians, not degrees. The value returned by the ATN function will be in radians.

To illustrate the use of these functions, type in and run the program given in activity 2.2. The purpose of line 20 in this program is to convert the angle A in degrees into its equivalent in radians.

Other useful functions in BASIC are the INT, ABS and SGN functions. INT returns the whole number part of any variable which is a positive decimal

```
10 INPUT A
20 LET A=3.14159/180*A
30 LET S=SIN(A)
40 PRINT S
50 LET C= COS(A)
60 PRINT C
70 LET T=TAN(A)
80 PRINT T
90 LET A1=ATN(T)
100 PRINT A1
110 END
```

Activity 2.2

```
10 INPUT X
20 LET Y=SGN(X)
30 PRINT Y
40 LET Y=ABS(X)
50 PRINT Y
60 LET Y=INT(X)
70 PRINT Y
80 END
```

Activity 2.3

number; but what happens if the variable is a negative decimal number ? ABS returns the absolute value of a number, that is, its numerical size irrespective of sign, while SGN returns +1, –1 or zero depending on whether the number is positive, negative or zero. Type in and run the program shown in activity 2.3. For the first run, input a positive whole number. For the second run, input a positive decimal fraction. Next, input a negative whole number and finally a negative decimal fraction.

A function which is very useful in programs which play games, or which simulate natural random events, is the random number generator. The random number generator is the

RND(D)

function, where D is a dummy variable, usually 1 or zero. The random numbers produced by RND are always positive numbers between zero and 1, so that numbers within specified ranges have to be generated by a statement such as

25 LET R = INT(RND(1)*1Ø) + 1

which will produce random numbers in the range 1 to 10.

Most versions of BASIC require that before the random number generator is used in a program, the word RANDOMIZE must occur as a program statement. The program shown in activity 2.4 gives an example using the random number generator.

```
10 Y = RND(1)
20 PRINT Y
30 Y = INT(RND(1)*10)
40 PRINT Y
50 Y = INT(RND(1)*10)+1
60 PRINT Y
70 Y = INT(RND(1)*100)+1
80 PRINT Y
90 END
```

Activity 2.4

Activity 3

General

```
10 PRINT"FAHRENHEIT TEMPERATURE ";
15 INPUT F
20 LET C=(F-32)*5/9
30 PRINT "EQUIVALENT TEMPERATURE IN DEGREES CENTIGRADE IS ";C
40 END
```

Activity 3.1

To make a program easier to understand there are two useful features of BASIC. The first of these is illustrated in activity 3.1. Type it in and then run it. You should see that the words enclosed in inverted commas are displayed on the screen. All characters enclosed in inverted commas after a PRINT instruction are called *literals* and are always printed exactly as they appear in the program. Amend the program with one or more additional lines of literals of your own. For example, you could add a new line in front of line 10 which gives the program a title and names the author.

Run the program with any amendments you have made and then amend it further in the following ways

(1) omit the ; at the end of line 10.
(2) replace the ; at the end of line 10 by a comma.
(3) replace the ; in line 30 by ,

You should be able to see that by judicious use of commas and semicolons you can alter the format of the results from your program. In all the subsequent programs in this book you will see that you can use punctuation to control the display of output. There are other, more complex, ways of doing this. These methods can safely be left until you have developed more skill in programming.

Now try activity 3.2 and notice the use of the REMark statement which adds comments into the program without affecting the running of the program. All it does is to add to the clarity of the program.

A PRINT statement on its own will simply cause the printing of a blank line. This is a very useful statement which again helps with the layout of computer output. If the output is to a printing (hard copy) device, the effect of a single PRINT statement is to cause *carriage return/line feed*.

```
10 REM***THIS PROGRAM ILLUSTRATES THE USE OF REM***
20 REM***STATEMENTS***
30 PRINT "THIS IS A HEADING"
40 PRINT "=================="
50 PRINT
60 REM***AN INPUT STATEMENT NOW FOLLOWS***
70 INPUT "TYPE IN A NUMBER ";P
80 LET Q=P*P
90 PRINT P;" SQUARED = ";Q
100 PRINT " THATS'S ALL FOLKS!"
110 PRINT "THIS IS THE END OF THE PROGRAM"
120 END
```

Activity 3.2

The use of the word INPUT followed by a literal, as in line 70 of activity 3.2, is a short-cut way of printing a request for input. A PRINT statement followed by an INPUT statement can be condensed into a single INPUT followed by a literal and then the input variable name. Lines 10 and 20 of activity 3.1 could be replaced by the single line

1Ø INPUT "FAHRENHEIT TEMPERATURE ?",F

Activity 4

General

This activity introduces you to the very important concept of decision statements or jumps. These are of two types:

(1) GO TO *nnn*

where *nnn* is a line number of an instruction in the program. A GO TO statement directs the execution of the program to a specific line which is not the next line in sequence. Remember that programs will always execute in line number order unless a jump instruction directs otherwise.

(2) IF. . . . . . . THEN . . . .

is a conditional jump instruction which is in the form of a test of a statement being true or false. On the result of this test there are two options open to the program. If the test fails – the statement is false – the next statement in sequence is carried out. If the test is true then the next specified instruction after the word THEN is executed.

25Ø IF X = 1 THEN 4ØØ

means that if the value of the variable X is equal to 1 then the next instruction to be carried out will be on line 400. If the value of X is not 1, then the line immediately following line 250 is the next to be carried out.

```
10 INPUT "METRES,CENTIMETRES ";M,C
20 LET M1=M+C/100
30 LET I=M1*39.37
40 LET F=INT(I/12)
50 LET I=I-12*F
60 PRINT M;" METRES ";C;" CENTIMETRES"
70 PRINT "CONVERT TO ";
80 IF F=0 THEN 100
90 PRINT F;"FEET";
100 PRINT I; "INCHES"
110 GOTO 10
120 END
```

Activity 4.1

Type in and run the program shown in activity 4.1. Notice how the program always loops back to line 10. The only way to interrupt the program, in order to stop it, is to halt the execution of the program by pressing the keys CONTROL and X or a RUN STOP key. This is a common way of stopping a program which has got into a loop from which there is no escape. It is not a particularly elegant way of stopping a program and so a method is needed to bring a program to a controlled halt. This is often done by testing an input number for a particular value. If this value is input then the program halts. If it is not, then the program can proceed round its loop until another number is input and tested. A commonly used value which can be tested to stop the program is –1, but any number will do. Put the additional statement

```
15 IF M = –1 THEN STOP
```

and run the program again. Once the value of –1 has been assigned to M the program will stop. Do not forget that this program always requires two numbers to be input. The first is –1 to stop the program but another number has to be input with it, although its value is quite unimportant since it is the value of M which is tested.

See if you can modify the program to cause the suppression of the value of M should it be zero in line 60, in the same way as the suppression of the printing of a zero number of feet was done in line 80.

If you have successfully completed the first activity, see if you can write your own program to convert English pounds into dollars using the current rate of exchange. Then see if you can modify your program to perform the conversion in either direction, that is, pounds to dollars, or dollars to pounds.

The tests we can use as part of an IF statement are usually an arithmetic comparison of two numbers and the kinds of comparison are of equality or non-equality. We can test to see if

	sign
(1) Two numbers are equal	=
(2) One number is greater than another	>
(3) One number is less than another	<
(4) One number is greater than or equal to another	>=
(5) One number is less than or equal to another	<=
(6) Two numbers are unequal	<>

Thus we could write tests of the form:

```
1ØØ IF X = Y THEN 2ØØ
```

or

1ØØ IF X > Y THEN 2ØØ

or

1ØØ IF X < Y THEN 2ØØ

or

1ØØ IF X > = Y THEN 2ØØ

or

1ØØ IF X < = Y THEN 2ØØ

or

1ØØ IF X <> Y THEN 2ØØ

Most versions of BASIC available on microcomputers make it possible to have any valid BASIC statement placed after the THEN part of a conditional jumps statement. This means that we could write

1ØØ IF X <> Y THEN LET X = Y

and this would mean that if the value of X and Y were not the same then the program would make them equal. Now try the program given in activity 4.2.

The final program in this activity is one which makes use of a number of features of BASIC dealt with so far. Activity 4.3 simulates the throwing of a six-sided die using the random number generator.

```
10 INPUT X,Y
20 IF X=Y THEN 60
30 IF X>Y THEN PRINT X;"IS THE LARGER"
40 IF X>Y THEN 60
50 IF X<Y THEN PRINT Y;"IS THE LARGER"
60 PRINT"THAT'S THE END"
70 END
```

Activity 4.2

```
10 K=0
30 Y=RND(1)
40 IF Y>.5 THEN 70
50 T=T+1
60 GOTO 80
70 H=H+1
80 K=K+1
90 IF K >= 1000 THEN 110
100 GOTO 30
110 PRINT "THERE WERE ";H;" HEADS AND ";T; "TAILS"
120 PRINT "OUT OF ";K;" THROWS"
130 END
```

Activity 4.3

Activity 5

General

In some programs we need to jump to particular parts according to the value of some variable. Many programs are written in such a way as to cause only sections of them to be executed during any single program run. The section branched to can be selected by using the statement

ON. . .GOTO. . .

Type in and run the program shown in activity 5.1. This program illustrates how the statement, called a *computed* GOTO, works. Input values of K which are 1, 2, 3 and 4 in turn.

```
10 INPUT K
20 ON K THEN GOTO 50,70,90
30 PRINT "THEN NUMBER YOU HAVE INPUT IS NOT AN INTEGER BETWEEN 1 & 3"
40 STOP
50 PRINT "K WAS EQUAL TO 1"
60 GOTO 10
70 PRINT "K WAS EQUAL TO 2"
80 GOTO 10
90 PRINT "K WAS EQUAL TO 3"
100 GOTO 10
110 END
```

Activity 5.1

The next step is to put the ON. . .GOTO. . . statement to work, and the program shown in activity 5.2 illustrates this.

```
10 PRINT " DO YOU REQUIRE A TABLE OF SQUARES,CUBES ";
20 PRINT " OR SQUARE ROOTS ?"
30 INPUT"TYPE IN 1,2, OR 3. 0 WILL STOP THE PROGRAM ";K
40 IF K=0 THEN STOP
50 ON K GOTO 80,140,200
60 PRINT "THE NUMBER MUST BE 1,2 OR 3"
70 GOTO 30
80 PRINT "TABLE OF SQUARES"
90 X=1
100 PRINT X;" SQUARED = ";X^2
110 X=X+1
120 IF X> 10 THEN 30
130 GOTO 100
140 PRINT "TABLE OF CUBES"
150 X=1
160 PRINT X;"CUBED = ";X^3
170 X=X+1
180 IF X>10 THEN 30
190 GOTO 160
200 PRINT "TABLE OF SQUARE ROOTS"
210 X=1
220 PRINT "SQUARE ROOT OF ";X;" = ";SQR(X)
230 X=X+1
240 IF X> 10 THEN 30
250 GOTO 220
260 END
```

Activity 5.2

Activity 6

General and Mathematical

The IF. . .THEN. . . statement (see activity 4) is a test based on the assertion that follows the word IF. The instruction following the word THEN is carried out only if the assertion is true. If it is false then the branching instruction is ignored. As well as the relational operators mentioned in activity 4, the equality and inequality relations, there are other *truth* assertions. There are three of these and they are AND, NOT and OR. These operators are put to work in activity 6.1

```
10 INPUT X,Y
20 IF X>0 AND Y>0 THEN 50
30 PRINT 'AT LEAST ONE NUMBER WAS NEGATIVE'
40 STOP
50 PRINT 'BOTH NUMBERS WERE POSITVE'
60 END
```

Activity 6.1

which you can type in and run, using the following input in turn

(1) 1,2
(2) –1,2·
(3) –1,–2
(4) 1,–2

Now replace line 20 with

20 IF X > 0 OR Y > 0 THEN 50

and lines 30 and 50 with

30 PRINT "BOTH NUMBERS ARE NEGATIVE"
50 PRINT "AT LEAST ONE NUMBER IS POSITIVE"

Then run the program with the data as before. Your results should clearly show what the effects of the AND and OR operators are. They, in fact, mean exactly what they say in the program.

The NOT assertion is rather more difficult to appreciate but the program given in activity 6.2 should help to show its use, although at this stage of your programming experience you may not be able to realise the full potential of such a feature of BASIC. Run this program with input values of 1, –1, 0 and 100 and then amend the program as shown in activity 6.3. Run this new program with the same set of data as you used for the running of activity 6.2.

```
10 INPUT X
20 IF NOT X <> 0 THEN 50
30 PRINT 'THE NUMBER WAS NON-ZERO'
40 STOP
50 PRINT 'THE NUMBER WAS ZERO'
60 STOP
```

Activity 6.2

```
10 INPUT X
20 IF X THEN 50
30 PRINT 'THE NUMBER WAS ZERO'
40 STOP
50 PRINT 'THE NUMBER WAS NOT EQUAL TO ZERO'
60 END
```

Activity 6.3

What is happening is that the *truth* value of X is being evaluated. This means that if X has the value of zero then the *truth* value of X is *false*. (False = zero, true = non-zero.) If X is zero then NOT X is *true*, and if X has a non-zero value then the truth value of NOT X is *false*. In fact, after every IF the assertion is tested for its truth value so that

IF X > Ø THEN. . . . .

has the assertion that X is greater than zero tested for its truth value. If the assertion 'X is greater than zero' is true, the THEN branch is executed. If the assertion 'X is greater than zero' is false, then the next statement in sequence is executed.

```
10 INPUT X
20 IF 0 < X < 1 THEN 50
30 PRINT 'AT LINE 30'
40 STOP
50 PRINT 'AT LINE 50'
```

Activity 6.4 (a)

```
10 INPUT X
20 IF 0 < X AND X < 1 THEN 50
30 PRINT 'AT LINE 30'
40 STOP
50 PRINT 'AT LINE 50'
```

Activity 6.4 (b)

Activity 6.4 is really in the form of a puzzle. The program is simple enough, and is intended to make a jump to line 50 if X lies between zero and 1, and to go to line 30 if X lies outside those limits. Activity 6.4a has the test written as a mathematician would tend to write it, since it is quite clear to him that

$0 < X < 1$

means that X should be greater than zero, but less than 1. Type in activity 6.4a, and run it with inputs of –1, 0, 0.51 and 10. Note the results. Are they what you would expect?

Now replace line 20 so that the program is as shown in activity 6.4b and rerun with the same data as before.

The puzzle is, why does one version work and the other not? A little exploration among the mathematics of truth tables will give a clue to the answer.

Activity 7

General

This activity is about a feature of BASIC which enables a series of related calculations to be performed in what is usually referred to as a *loop*. An example of a loop was used in activity 5.2 where a set of tables of squares, cubes and square roots were printed for a set number of numbers. The loops were generated by IF. . .THEN. . . and GO TO statements. A neater way of doing this is by using a FOR. . . .NEXT. . . loop. Type in and run the program shown in activity 7.1. When you run the program you should see that the values of X which are printed are 0, 2, 4, 6, 8 and 10. This is the meaning of the statement in line 10 which says that the value of X must start at zero and go up to 10 in steps of 2. Line 40 defines the end of the loop and it is at this point that the value of X is tested for its terminal value, in this case 10, and the program returned to line 10 if the terminal value has not yet been reached. If the terminal value has been reached, then the program continues from line 50 and drops out of the loop.

```
10 FOR X=0 TO 10 STEP 2
20 LET Y=X^2
30 PRINT X;Y
40 NEXT X
50 END
```

Activity 7.1

Amend the program so that the step size is 0.5 instead of 2 and run it again. Then amend the program so that it first of all requests the step size before entering the loop; in other words you have to amend line 10 so that a variable name replaces the 2 or the 0.5. A value can be given to that variable by an INPUT statement on the previous line. Run the program again and finally amend it so that the starting value, the target value and the step size are all requested before the loop is entered. By doing this you can control exactly how many times, and in what step size, the loop is executed.

We can use FOR. . .NEXT. . . loops as the basis for a large number of useful programs. One of these is the program shown in activity 7.2. This program accumulates the sum of a series of numbers which are input into RAM one at a time. This program requires us to know, in advance, how many numbers are to be summed. Note that line 30 does not include the word STEP. This is because

```
10 INPUT"HOW MANY ITEMS ";N
20 PRINT "NOW INPUT THE NUMBERS ONE AT A TIME"
30 LET T=0
40 FOR C=1 TO N
50 INPUT X
60 LET T=T+X
70 NEXT C
80 PRINT "THE TOTAL IS ";T
90 END
```

Activity 7.2

BASIC allows us to omit the step size if it is equal to 1. Run the program with input of your own choice and do not forget to check that the answer is correct.

```
10 LET T=0
20 PRINT "TYPE IN THE NUMBERS ONE AT A TIME. TYPE -1 TO FINISH"
30 FOR C=0 TO 1000
40 INPUT X
50 IF X=-1 THEN 80
60 LET T=T+X
70 NEXT C
80 PRINT "TOTAL OF ";C;" NUMBERS WAS ";T
90 STOP
```

Activity 7.3

Activity 7.3 shows a variation of the previous program which can be used if the number of items in the list of numbers being summed is not known. The program uses the device of a *flag* to signal that the end of the list has been reached. In this case the flag is –1, but any number could be used so long as it did not occur in the list. When the flag is recognised the program drops out of the loop and the total is printed. Notice that in both these programs the loop counter counts the number of input items processed by the loop. Notice the very important line in both these examples which accumulates the total in a variable called T (LET T = T + X). What this line is saying is that the input variable value is to be added to the current value of T, and the result returned to the location occupied by the variable T; thus T keeps a running total.

Activity 8

General

```
10 LET T=0
20 FOR C=0 TO 1000
30 READ X
40 IF X=-1 THEN 80
50 LET T=T+X
60 NEXT C
70 DATA 5,6,8,9,7,4,1,2,-1
80 PRINT "TOTAL OF ";C;" NUMBERS WAS ";T
90 STOP
```

Activity 8.1

Type in and run the program listed in activity 8.1. Notice that it is almost identical to activity 7.3. The difference between the two programs is that the word INPUT has been replaced by the word READ and a DATA line has been added. When the program runs there is no ? prompt to ask you to type in the data at the keyboard. All the numbers to be input into the program already reside in the DATA line and are picked off, one by one, by the READ instruction. Every time the READ instruction is executed a number of variables are read off the DATA list. The number of variables in the list after the READ tell us the number of items read each time that statement is executed. The program runs far quicker than if we had used INPUT rather than READ, since the program does not have to wait for you to type numbers in. A program can have any number of DATA lines and the numbers held in these lines are read off in sequence. Add extra data to your program by adding the lines

```
65 DATA 4, 5, 3, 6, 7, 8, 9, 23, 2, 6, 45, 6, 7, 9, 1Ø
68 DATA 6.7, 8.3, 4, 56, 78, 2.3, 55, 2.2, 16.9
```

and run the program again.

Activity 8.1 uses the facility of reading data from a series of DATA statements, which incidentally can be placed anywhere in the program. There are occasions when the same data need to be read more than once by a program. In this case, there is the RESTORE statement which causes the next READ to take place from the beginning of the first DATA line, irrespective of where the last data item was read from. Activity 8.2 illustrates a simple example of the use of the RESTORE statement. Note also that the last item in the DATA list is never read, since the program instructions say that only the first five, and then

```
10 FOR I=1 TO 5
20 READ X
30 PRINT X;
40 NEXT I
50 RESTORE
60 PRINT
70 FOR I = 1 TO 10
80 READ X
90 PRINT X;
100 NEXT I
110 DATA 4,3,2,-9,8,6,2,1,-4,45,100
120 END
```

Activity 8.2

the first ten, data items are to be read. As there are 11 data items in the DATA line, the last one will never be read.

Activity 9

General

The following short activity will get you familiar with three very useful functions associated with the layout of output on the video screen or printer, should your system have one. The functions are TAB, SPC and POS.

TAB causes the position of the next printed character to be specified. Try the program given in activity 9.1.

```
10 INPUT A,B,C
20 PRINT A;TAB(10);B;TAB(20);C
30 PRINT A;TAB(20);B;TAB(30);C
40 PRINT TAB(10);A;TAB(20);B;TAB(30);C
50 FOR I = 1 TO 10
60 PRINT TAB(I);A;TAB(I+10);B;TAB(I+20);C
70 NEXT I
80 END
```

Activity 9.1

SPC causes a specified number of spaces to be placed between successive items of output. The program in activity 9.2 demonstrates this feature.

```
10 INPUT A,B,C
20 PRINT A;SPC(5);B;SPC(5);C
30 FOR I = 1 TO 10
40 PRINT SPC(I);A;SPC(I);B;SPC(I);C
50 NEXT I
60 END
```

Activity 9.2

POS records the position of the current character being printed. A statement using POS always has to have a dummy variable as the argument of POS. For example in the statement

N = POS(X)

the X has no part in the program as it is merely a dummy variable in much the same way that in some versions of BASIC the argument of the RND function is a dummy variable.

Activity 10

Mathematical

```
10 DEF FNA(X)=INT(LOG(ABS(X))/LOG(10))
20 DEF FNB(X)=INT(LOG(0.1+ABS(X))/(LOG(10))
30 READ X
40 IF X=1E+10 THEN STOP
50 LET T=10
60 IF ABS(X)<0.1 THEN 90
70 PRINT TAB(T-FNA(X));X
80 GOTO 30
90 PRINT TAB(T-FNB(X));X
100 GOTO 30
110 DATA 45,678.2,222,-.1,33.4,-88.9
120 DATA 44678,99.07,-345.67,786,234.009
130 DATA 1E+10
140 END
```

Activity 10.1

Type in and run the program shown in activity 10.1. Note that lines 10 and 20 contain two new BASIC statements. These are called *user-defined* functions, and their particular purpose in this program is to cause the printing of numbers in the DATA lines in such a way that their decimal points lie under one another; BASIC usually aligns the first characters, not the decimal points. The FN functions at the beginning of the program define what the functions are and make it possible for complicated functions to be referred to by a name rather than having to be typed in laboriously every time they are to be used. Up to 26 FN functions can be defined, known as FNA, FNB, FNC, etc.

```
10 DEF FNF(T)=COS(2*T+0.5)+SIN(3*T-1)
20 FOR A = 0 TO 6 STEP .25
30 IF FNF(A)>.5 THEN 50
40 IF FNF(A)<.5 THEN 60
50 PRINT A;FNF(A)
60 NEXT A
70 END
```

Activity 10.2

The program in activity 10.2 illustrates another example of an FN function being used. Note that the variable in brackets after the function name is the variable used on the right hand side in the definition of the function. Every time the function is referred to in the program its value is calculated for that value of the variable enclosed in the brackets. If we have

```
10 DEF FNC(X) = X↑2 + 4*X – 3
```

then

```
5Ø LET Z = FNC(T)
```

will evaluate the expression defined as FNC for the current value of T being assigned to the variable in the definition. The final value of the function is assigned to the variable Z. Notice that in most versions of BASIC only one variable is allowed in a function definition.

Activity 11

General and Mathematical

This activity is about the use of lists of numbers held in the computer's memory. A list is referred to by any valid variable name, and any item held in that list is located by a number in brackets after that variable name. For example, a list could be called by the name K, and K(7) would refer to the seventh item in that list. Every list has to be DIMensioned so that storage space can be reserved for it in RAM. Try the program listed in activity 11.1. The DIM statement reserves the number of locations to be allocated to the list specified by the number in brackets after the variable name. In this case the list A is to hold ten separate numbers referred to as A(1), A(2) . . . . A(10).

```
10 DIM A(10)
20 FOR I = 1 TO 10
30 INPUT A(I)
40 NEXT I
50 FOR I = 1 TO 10
60 PRINT A(I);
70 NEXT I
80 END
```

Activity 11.1

When you have run the program successfully, replace line 60 with the line

```
6Ø PRINT A(I)*2
```

and run the program again. When you have done that, insert the following lines into the program

```
45 LET T = Ø
6Ø LET T = T + A(I)
75 PRINT T;T/1Ø
```

and run the program again. When you have tried that version of the program you should be able to insert a line between lines 70 and 75 which will explain the nature of the answers which follow. The next thing to do is to type in the lines

```
46 LET S = Ø
61 LET S = S + A(I)↑2
76 LET D = SQR(S/1Ø – (T/1Ø)↑2)
77 PRINT D
```

Run the program as it now appears and then see if you can write a program which will calculate the mean, and the standard deviation, of any number of numbers.

```
10 DIM L(100)
20 FOR I=1 TO 100
30 READ L(I)
40 IF L(I)=999 THEN 60
50 NEXT I
60 F=0
70 FOR K=1 TO I-1
80 IF L(K)>L(K+1) THEN 120
90 NEXT K
100 IF F=0 THEN 170
110 GOTO 60
120 T=L(K)
130 L(K)=L(K+1)
140 L(K+1)=T
150 F=1
160 GOTO 90
170 FOR J=1 TO I-1
180 PRINT L(J);
190 NEXT J
200 STOP
210 DATA 56,23,41,87,2,5,36,87,12,112,90
220 DATA 21,64,15,77,54,100,23,52,45,88,32
240 DATA 4,7,25,34,41,12,45,999
250 END
```

Activity 11.2

Activity 11.2 shows an example of a very important computer application, that of sorting a list of numbers into numerical order. The program works by scanning the contents of a list, and swapping over any pair of numbers where the first number of the pair is greater than the second number. The list is repeatedly scanned until the situation arises that no swaps are necessary. At that point the sort is complete.

```
10 DIM L(100)
20 FOR I=1 TO 100
30 READ L(I)
40 IF L(I)=999 THEN 60
50 NEXT I
60 H=1
70 L=1E20
80 FOR J=1 TO I-1
90 IF L(J)=1E20 THEN 110
100 IF L>L(J) THEN 170
110 NEXT J
120 PRINT L;
130 H=H+1
140 IF H=I THEN STOP
150 L(K)=1E20
160 GOTO 70
170 K=J
180 L=L(J)
190 GOTO 110
200 STOP
210 DATA 56,23,41,87,2,5,36,87,12,112,90
220 DATA 21,64,15,77,54,100,23,52,45,88,32
240 DATA 4,7,25,34,41,12,45,999
250 END
```

Activity 11.3

The program in activity 11.3 illustrates another method of sorting numbers held in a list. It is of interest to compare the relative speeds with which this program and the previous one sort the same list of numbers. Their relative speeds show up, of course, only when the list is large. You might like to examine the programs and find a way (there are several), by which the sorting processes can be speeded up.

```
10 DIM L(100)
20 FOR I = 1 TO 100
30 READ L(I)
40 IF L(I)=999 THEN 60
50 NEXT I
60 L=L(1)
70 H=L(1)
80 FOR J=2 TO I-1
90 IF L>L(J) THEN 140
100 IF H<L(J) THEN 160
110 NEXT J
120 PRINT "THE LARGEST NUMBER IS ";H;" AND THE SMALLEST NUMBER IS ";L
130 STOP
140 L=L(J)
150 GOTO 110
160 H=L(J)
170 GOTO 110
180 DATA 12,65,44,19,52,78,31,55,78,21
190 DATA 2,6,99,45,55,74,32,12,8,66,999
200 END
```

Activity 11.4

A simple program which also handles a list is shown in activity 11.4. In this example the largest and smallest numbers in a list are discovered. Finally in this section activity 11.5 shows an example of a program which you will see contains the use of many of the features covered in the activities so far. It is a simple game in which the object is to hit a target 2000 metres away.

```
10 K=0
20 Z=1
30 N=2000
40 PRINT"RANGE OF TARGET = ";N;" METRES"
50 INPUT"VELOCITY IN METRES PER SECOND ";V
60 IF K=1 THEN 100
70 INPUT"PROJECTION HEIGHT ABOVE GROUND IN METRES = ";H
80 IF K=2 THEN 100
90 INPUT"ANGLE OF PROJECTION TO THE HORIZONTAL IN DEGREES ";A
100 B=A/57.3
110 C=TAN(B)
120 D=.5*(1+COS(2*B))
130 E=9.81/(2*(V^2)*D)
140 X=(C+SQR(C^2+4*E*H))/(2*E)
150 X(Z)=X
160 GOTO 430
170 IF ABS(N-X)<1 THEN 300
180 IF X>N THEN 240
190 F=N-X
200 PRINT
210 PRINT"PROJECTILE FELL ";F;" METRES SHORT"
220 PRINT
230 GOTO 330
240 G=X-N
250 PRINT
260 PRINT"THE PROJECTILE FELL ";G;" METRES BEYOND TARGET"
270 PRINT
280 GOTO 330
290 PRINT
300 PRINT"******"
310 PRINT"*BANG*";SPC(10);"GOOD SHOT!"
320 PRINT"******"
330 INPUT"DO YOU WISH TO ALTER ANY VALUES - YES=1,NO=0";P
```

```
340 IF P=1 THEN 360
350 IF P=0 THEN 420
360 Z=Z+1
370 IF Z=4 THEN 400
380 INPUT"TO CHANGE VELOCITY TYPE 1,HEIGHT TYPE,2,ELEVATION TYPE 3 ";K
390 ON K GOTO 50,70,90
400 PRINT"SORRY YOU HAVE HAD THREE TRIES"
410 PRINT"YOUR RESULTS WERE :- ";X(1);X(2);X(3)
420 GOTO 540
430 X1=C/(2*E)
440 Y1=X1*C-E*((X1)^2+H)
450 FOR P=0 TO N STEP N/20
460 Y=P*C-E*(P^2)+H
470 IF Y<0 THEN 530
480 Q=INT((Y/Y1)*30)
490 R=ABS(Q)
500 IF R=0 THEN LET R=1
510 PRINT":";TAB(R);"*"
520 NEXT P
530 GOTO 170
540 E=(4*(H+(N*C)))/(N^2*4)
550 V2=SQR((9.81)/(D*E*2))
560 PRINT"THE CORRECT DATA FOR A HIT WOULD BE:-"
570 PRINT"VELOCITY - ";V2;" METRES PER SECOND"
580 PRINT"PROJECTION HEIGHT OF ";H;" METRES"
590 PRINT"ANGLE OF PROJECTION ";A;" DEGREES"
600 END
```

Activity 11.5

Activity 12

General

Activity 11 was about lists of numbers, and this activity takes the idea one dimension further. It deals with tables, two dimensional lists, sometimes known as arrays. Elements of an array have to be indexed by two numbers; the first of these identifies the row, and the second the column within that row, where the element is to be found. Thus L(2, 3) refers to the number held in the third column of the second row of the array called L. Type in and run the program shown in activity 12.1. When you have successfully run that, try the program with line 110 omitted, and note the effect this has on the way the output is displayed on the screen.

```
10 DIM X(3,4)
20 FOR I = 1 TO 3
30 FOR J = 1 TO 4
40 INPUT X(I,J)
50 NEXT J
60 NEXT I
70 FOR I = 1 TO 3
80 FOR J = 1 TO 4
90 PRINT X(I,J);
100 NEXT J
110 PRINT
120 NEXT I
130 END
```

Activity 12.1

After you have run the program, replace line 110 and insert the three extra lines

```
75 LET T = Ø
9Ø LET T = T + X(I, J)
11Ø PRINT T
```

and note the effect these lines have on the program.

The next program to try is in activity 12.2, which shows an example of an array put to use. In the program an array called R is used to hold the information regarding the status of a number of teams in a football league. The first column of the array holds the number of matches played, the second holds the number of matches won, the third the number of matches lost and the fourth the number of drawn games. The last three columns hold the number of goals scored by the team, the number of goals scored against the team and the number

```
10 DIM R(10,7)
20 INPUT T1,T2,G1,G2
30 IF T1=-1 THEN 290
40 R(T1,1)=R(T1,1)+1
50 R(T2,1)=R(T2,1)+1
60 IF G1=G2 THEN 150
70 IF G1>G2 THEN 220
80 R(T1,3)=R(T1,3)+1
90 R(T1,5)=R(T1,5)+G1
100 R(T1,6)=R(T1,6)+G2
110 R(T2,2)=R(T2,2)+1
120 R(T2,6)=R(T2,6)+G1
130 R(T2,5)=R(T2,5)+G2
140 GOTO 20
150 R(T1,4)=R(T1,4)+1
160 R(T2,4)=R(T2,4)+1
170 R(T2,5)=R(T2,5)+G2
180 R(T2,6)=R(T2,6)+G1
190 R(T1,5)=R(T1,5)+G1
200 R(T1,6)=R(T1,6)+G2
210 GOTO 20
220 R(T1,2)=R(T1,2)+1
230 R(T2,6)=R(T2,6)+G1
240 R(T2,5)=R(T2,5)+G2
250 R(T2,3)=R(T2,3)+1
260 R(T1,5)=R(T1,5)+G1
270 R(T1,6)=R(T1,6)+G2
280 GOTO 20
290 PRINT"TEAM  P    W     L     D   FOR AGT PTS"
300 PRINT"======================================"
310 FOR I = 1 TO 10
320 PRINT I;
330 PRINT SPC(2);R(I,1);SPC(2);R(I,2);
340 PRINT SPC(2);R(I,3);SPC(2);R(I,4);
350 PRINT SPC(2);R(I,5);SPC(2);R(I,6);
360 PRINT SPC(2);R(I,7)
370 NEXT I
```

Activity 12.2

of points awarded to a team so far, according to a rule, say, two for a win and one for a draw. The only input required is a pair of numbers to identify the teams, home team first, and a pair of numbers giving the number of goals scored by the teams, home team first. The program then updates the relevant rows of the array, one row per team involved, and requests another result. When the results are complete, a team number of –1 is input to signify the end of the data, and the full position of the league table is printed out. The program has been deliberately left incomplete so that the insertion of the points column can be put in by you. If you can do that with the minimum of effort, you can be sure that you are getting to understand about arrays.

Activity 13

General

The manipulation of what are called *strings* in BASIC forms a very important part of the use of this language. String variables are distinguished from numeric variables by the addition of a dollar sign, $, after the variable name. String variables are different from numeric variables in the amount of storage they take up; string variables take up one byte per character, compared with numerical data which take up at least two bytes. In addition, a string variable can be any one of the characters available on your keyboard whether they be digits, letters of the alphabet or special characters. Numeric variables can only be, as the name implies, numbers.

Before a string can be used in a program, space usually has to be reserved for it either by means of a DIM statement, since a string is a list of characters, or a CLEAR statement. A clear statement can either be of the form

```
1Ø CLEAR
```

or

```
1Ø CLEAR 3ØØ
```

where the number indicates the number of bytes to be reserved for string variables. In some versions of BASIC the instruction is

```
1Ø STRING = 3ØØ
```

Type in and run the program shown in activity 13.1. Note how in line 20 the contents of the string called A$ are enclosed in quotation marks. String variables

```
10 A$="DEMONSTRATION"
20 INPUT B$
30 PRINT A$,B$
40 C$=A$+B$
50 PRINT C$
70 C$=A$+"  "+B$
80 PRINT C$
90 END
```

Activity 13.1

can be enclosed in quotes so that BASIC can detect the correct way to store them. When you run the program see what happens when you respond to the ? in the first run with

"STRING"

and in the second run with

STRING

Notice the statement in line 40 of the program which is the only kind of operation which can be performed on a string; that of *concatenation* where one string is appended to another. If you wish to replace line 20 with any statement which assigns a particular string to A$ then that string must be enclosed in quotes.

Now we come to the concept of a *substring*. A substring is a portion of a string, and in order to access substrings with a string we use the LEFT$, RIGHT$ and MID$ keywords. These work as follows

LEFT$(A$, X) accesses the first X characters of the string A$.
RIGHT$(A$, X) accesses the last X characters of the string A$.
MID$(A$, X, Y) accesses the substring within A$ starting at the Xth character and containing Y characters from that point.

This is very useful when a single character is to be picked out from a string when MID$(A$, 3, 1) will pick out the character "C" from the string A$ containing the characters "MICRO".

Now try the program listed in activity 13.2 which uses the three substring keywords.

```
20 A$="MICROCOMPUTER"
30 INPUT A,B
40 IF A>13 OR B>13 THEN 30
50 B$=LEFT$(A$,A)
60 PRINT B$
70 B$=RIGHT$(A$,B)
80 PRINT B$
90 B$=MID$(A$,A,B)
100 PRINT B$
110 B$=MID$(A$,B,1)
120 PRINT B$
130 END
```

Activity 13.2

```
20 FOR I = 1 TO 10
30 INPUT A$(I)
40 NEXT I
50 INPUT "TYPE ANY NUMBER BETWEEN 1 & 10 ";N
60 PRINT A$(N)
70 STOP
80 END
```

Activity 13.3

The program in activity 13.3 illustrates the use of lists of strings. In the same way as we can have a variable name referring to a list, and subscripting the name to indicate a particular item in that list, we can have a list of strings. The list name can be any valid string name and the subscript refers to a particular string in the list. Hence, we can have lists of strings and indeed, arrays of strings.

```
20 DIM N$(50)
30 READ N
40 FOR I=1 TO N
50 READ N$(I)
60 NEXT I
70 FOR I = 1 TO N
80 FOR J = 1 TO N-1
90 IF N$(J)<=N$(J+1) THEN 130
100 A$=N$(J)
110 N$(J)=N$(J+1)
120 N$(J+1)=A$
130 NEXT J
140 NEXT I
150 FOR I = 1 TO N
160 PRINT N$(I)
170 NEXT I
180 STOP
190 DATA 20
200 DATA TOM,DICK,HARRY,BILL,CHARLIE,FRED
210 DATA TREVOR,CLARENCE,FRANK,EDDIE,DENNIS,ERNIE
220 DATA EDWARD,ROY,PADDY,JOHN,STANLEY,BRIAN
230 DATA MALCOLM,DAVID
```

Activity 13.4

Activity 13.4 is a program which will enable you to sort a list of names held in a string list, in a similar way to the program which sorted a list of numbers in activity 11.2. Note that the dimension statement on line 10 allocates space for a maximum of 50 elements to be stored in the string list called **N$**. Similarly in activity 13.5 an array of strings called **P$** is dimensioned in line 20. This activity illustrates the selection and modification of strings held in an array. Note again the similarity between this program and the one shown in activity 12.1.

```
20 DIM P$(4,4)
30 FOR I = 1 TO 4
40 FOR J = 1 TO 4
50 READ P$(I,J)
60 NEXT J
70 NEXT I
80 FOR I = 1 TO 4
90 FOR J = 1 TO 4
100 PRINT P$(I,J);" ";
110 NEXT J
120 PRINT
130 NEXT I
140 INPUT"WHICH NAME DO YOU WISH TO CHANGE ";A$
150 IF A$="NONE" THEN STOP
160 INPUT "WHAT IS THE NEW NAME TO BE ";B$
170 FOR I = 1 TO 4
180 FOR J = 1 TO 4
190 IF P$(I,J)=A$ THEN 280
200 NEXT J
210 NEXT I
220 PRINT "NAME NOT FOUND"
230 GOTO 140
240 DATA TOM,DICK,HARRY,FRED
250 DATA JO,JERRY,MAVIS,ARTHUR
260 DATA MARY,BILL,JENNY,PETER
270 DATA TIM,PADDY,ARNOLD,ROGER
280 P$(I,J)=B$
290 GOTO 80
```

Activity 13.5

```
20 INPUT M$
30 FOR I = 1 TO LEN(M$)
40 IF MID$(M$,I,1)='R' THEN 80
50 NEXT I
60 PRINT 'THERE IS NO R IN THE MONTH'
70 STOP
80 PRINT 'THERE IS AN R IN THE MONTH'
90 STOP
```

Activity 13.6

In activity 13.6 is a program which discovers whether there is an 'R' in the month, and uses the LEN function. LEN(A$) will give the length of the string A$, which is the number of characters it contains. All the program does is to search through the string M$ to see if any of the characters in it match the single character "R".

```
20 INPUT I$
30 F=0
40 A$='AEIOU'
50 PRINT 'INPUT STRING WAS ';I$
60 FOR I = 1 TO LEN(I$)
70 FOR J = 1 TO 5
80 IF MID$(A$,J,1)=MID$(I$,I,1) THEN 130
90 NEXT J
100 NEXT I
110 IF F=0 THEN PRINT 'NO VOWELS FOUND'
120 STOP
130 PRINT 'VOWEL ';MID$(A$,J,1);' FOUND'
140 F=1
150 GOTO 90
160 END
```

Activity 13.7

The matching of one string, or substring, against another is illustrated again in activity 13.7, where a string is searched for vowels. Each character in the input string is tested against each of the five vowels in the string A$ in turn, hence the two loops, one inside the other.

```
10 REM THIS PROGRAM CONVERTS A NUMBER
15 REM IN ANY BASE FROM 2 TO 16 BACK TO BASE 10
20 INPUT I$
30 A$='0123456789ABCDEF'
40 INPUT 'WHAT BASE WAS THAT ';B
50 N=0
60 FOR I = 1 TO LEN(I$)
70 IF MID$(I$,I,1)>MID$(A$,B,1) THEN PRINT'INVALID NUMBER'
80 IF MID$(I$,I,1)>MID$(A$,B,1) THEN 20
90 NEXT I
100 FOR I = LEN(I$) TO 1 STEP -1
110 D$=MID$(I$,I,1)
120 GOSUB 160
130 NEXT I
140 PRINTN
150 STOP
160 FOR J = 1 TO B
170 IF D$=MID$(A$,J,1) THEN LET K=J-1
180 NEXT J
190 N=N+K*B^(LEN(I$)-I)
200 RETURN
210 STOP
```

Activity 13.8

The next program, shown in activity 13.8, uses the VAL statement which converts a string variable into its numerical equivalent. For example, the statements

6Ø LET G$ = "1234"
7Ø LET G = VAL(G$)

will give to the numeric variable G the value of 1234. This statement is used in activities 13.8 and 13.9, one of which converts a decimal number into a number expressed in any base from 2 to 16, and the other performs the reverse operation.

```
10 REM THIS PROGRAM CONVERTS A DECIMAL
15 REM NUMBER TO ANY BASE FROM 2 TO 16
20 P=1
30 A$='0123456789ABCDEF'
40 INPUT I$
50 INPUT 'BASE ';B
60 O$='
70 T=VAL(I$)
80 FOR K=1 TO 100
90 T1=T/B
100 IF INT(T1)=T1 THEN O=0
110 IF INT(T1)=T1 THEN 160
120 O=T-INT(T1)*B
130 B$=MID$(A$,O+1,1)
140 O$=O$+B$
150 GOTO 180
160 B$='0'
170 O$=O$+B$
180 T=INT(T1)
190 IF T=0 THEN 220
200 P=P+1
210 NEXT K
220 FOR J=LEN(O$) TO 1 STEP -1
230 IF MID$(O$,J,1)=' ' THEN 250
240 PRINT MID$(O$,J,1);
250 NEXT J
260 STOP
```

Activity 13.9

The final activity, activity 13.10, uses strings to produce the product of two numbers to a very high degree of accuracy by giving the answer to a large number of significant figures, an accuracy not given in ordinary multiplication in BASIC, where six or eight significant figures are the best we can obtain.

```
10 REM THIS PROGRAM MULIPLIES TWO NUMBERS TOGETHER TO VERY GREAT ACCURACY
20 DIM U(265),V(132),W(132)
30 F$='0123456789'
40 INPUT'FIRST NUMBER ';A$
50 INPUT'SECOND NUMBER ';B$
60 Q=LEN(A$)
70 P=LEN(B$)
80 FOR I=1 TO Q+P
90 U(I)=0
100 NEXT I
110 FOR J=Q TO 1 STEP -1
120 C$=MID$(A$,Q-J+1,1)
130 FOR J1 = 1 TO 10
140 S$=MID$(F$,J1,1)
150 IF S$=C$ THEN 170
160 GOTO 180
170 V(J)=J1-1
180 NEXT J1
190 NEXT J
200 FOR K=P TO 1 STEP -1
```

```
210 D$=MID$(B$,P-K+1,1)
220 FOR K1=1 TO 10
230 T$=MID$(F$,K1,1)
240 IF T$=D$ THEN 260
250 GOTO 270
260 W(K)=K1-1
270 NEXT K1
280 NEXT K
290 FOR M=1 TO P
300 FOR N=1 TO Q
310 U(M+N-1)=U(M+N-1)+(V(N)*W(M))
320 IF U(M+N-1)>9 THEN LET U(M+N)=U(M+N)+INT(U(M+N-1)/10)
330 IF U(M+N-1)>9 THEN LET U(M+N-1)=U(M+N-1)-(INT(U(M+N-1)/10)*10)
340 NEXT N
350 NEXT M
360 PRINT"THEIR PRODUCT IS ";
370 Z$=""
380 FOR O=P+Q TO 1 STEP -1
390 FOR O1 = 0 TO 9
400 IF U(O)=O1 THEN 420
410 GOTO 440
420 E$=MID$(F$,O1+1,1)
430 Z$=Z$+E$
440 NEXT O1
450 NEXT O
460 IF LEFT$(Z$,1)="0" THEN PRINT RIGHT$(Z$,LEN(Z$)-1)
470 IF LEFT$(Z$,1)="0" THEN STOP
480 PRINTZ$
490 END
```

Activity 13.10

Activity 14

General

All high level computer languages use subroutines in one form or another, and BASIC is no exception. A subroutine enables a breakout to be made from the main stream of a program in order that a specialised routine may be performed.

```
10 PRINT "THIS PROGRAM DEMONSTRATES THE USE OF SUBROUTINES"
20 GOSUB 70
25 PRINT "I'M AT LINE 25"
30 GOSUB 100
35 PRINT "I'M AT LINE 35"
40 GOSUB 100
45 PRINT "I'M AT LINE 45"
50 GOSUB 70
55 PRINT "I'M AT LINE 55"
60 STOP
65 REM **SUBROUTINE 1**
70 PRINT "I'M AT LINE 70"
80 RETURN
90 REM **SUBROUTINE 2**
100 PRINT "I'M AT LINE 100"
110 RETURN
120 END
```

Activity 14.1

Once this routine is finished, the next instruction after that which caused the branch to the subroutine is performed. A simple example of a subroutine is the square root subroutine, which is called whenever the SQR function is used in BASIC. In this case the manufacturer has provided a routine to calculate square roots which is invoked whenever the need arises. We can write out our own subroutines in BASIC, and activity 14.1 shows an example of this. The branch to the subroutine itself is made by the

GOSUB *nnn*

instruction, where *nnn* is line number of the start of the subroutine. The return to the line following the GOSUB is made by the single instruction

RETURN

A more useful program which uses a pair of subroutines is shown in activity 14.2. In this example the branch to one or other of the subroutines is made as a

```
10 PRINT 'THIS PROGRAM CONVERTS POUNDS TO DOLLARS & VICE VERSA'
20 PRINT 'HOW MANY DOLLARS TO THE POUND ';
30 INPUT D1
40 PRINT 'POUNDS TO DOLLARS - YES OR NO - PRESS RETURN TO STOP PROGRAM '
50 INPUT A$
60 IF A$='YES' THEN GOSUB 100
70 IF A$='NO' THEN GOSUB 150
80 IF A$='' THEN STOP
90 GOTO 40
100 REM**SUBROUTINE TO CONVERT POUNDS TO DOLLARS**
110 INPUT 'HOW MANY POUNDS ';P
120 D=P*D1
130 PRINT '= ';D;' DOLLARS'
140 RETURN
150 REM**SUBROUTINE TO CONVERT DOLLARS TO POUNDS**
160 INPUT 'HOW MANY DOLLARS ';D
170 P=D/D1
180 PRINT '= ';P;' POUNDS'
190 RETURN
200 END
```

Activity 14.2

result of the answer to the question being "YES" or "NO". When you have successfully run this program try writing your own program which will convert ^{o}F to ^{o}C, and *vice versa*.

The activity which comes next, activity 14.3, is a program which contains no calculations at all. It is a number of simple logical tests which cause three numbers to be arranged in ascending order. Notice that it uses two subroutines, with REM statements to explain their purpose. Without them the program would be much longer than it is. This is because the same subroutines are used to swap over various pairs of numbers in turn.

```
10 INPUT A,B,C
20 IF A>B THEN LET X=A
30 IF A>B THEN LET Y=B
40 IF A>B THEN GOSUB 170
50 IF A>B THEN GOSUB 220
60 IF B>C THEN LET X=B
70 IF B>C THEN LET Y=C
80 IF B>C THEN GOSUB 170
90 IF B>C THEN GOSUB 260
100 IF A>B THEN LET X=A
110 IF A>B THEN LET Y=B
120 IF A>B THEN GOSUB 170
130 IF A>B THEN GOSUB 220
140 PRINT A;B;C
150 STOP
160 REM***SWAPPING SUBROUTINE***
170 T=X
180 X=Y
190 Y=T
200 RETURN
210 REM***REASSIGNMENT OF VALUES OF A & B ***
220 A=X
230 B=Y
235 RETURN
240 REM***REASSIGNMENT OF VALUES OF B & C ***
260 B=X
270 C=Y
280 RETURN
```

Activity 14.3

Just as activity 5.2 caused tables of squares, cubes or square roots to be calculated and printed, so activity 14.4 does the same thing using the

ON K GOSUB . . . .

instruction which works in a similar manner to the

ON K THEN GO TO . . . . .

instruction. The two differ by the fact that whenever a subroutine is used an automatic return is made to the program line immediately following the line which called the subroutine. A GOTO, however, implies a complete change of direction of the logic. A subroutine is just a temporary diversion, like looking up a fact in a reference book, before returning to the main stream of the program.

```
10 PRINT"DO YOU REQUIRE A TABLE OF SQUARES, CUBES ";
20 PRINT"OR SQUARE ROOTS ?"
30 INPUT"TYPE IN 1,2 OR 3. 0 WILL STOP THE PROGRAM";K
40 IF K=0 THEN STOP
50 ON K THEN GOSUB 70,130,190
60 GOTO 30
70 PRINT"TABLE OF SQUARES"
80 X=1
90 PRINTX;"SQUARED = ";X^2
100 X=X+1
110 IF X>10 THEN RETURN
120 GOTO 90
130 PRINT "TABLE OF CUBES"
140 X=1
150 PRINT X;"CUBED = ";X^3
160 X=X+1
170 IF X>10 THEN RETURN
180 GOTO 150
190 PRINT "TABLE OF SQUARE ROOTS"
200 X=1
210 PRINT "SQUARE ROOT OF ";X;"= ";SQR(X)
220 X=X+1
230 IF X>10 THEN RETURN
240 GOTO 210
250 END
```

Activity 14.4

Activity 15

Business

If your microcomputer possesses a backing store, either in the form of tape cassettes or discs, then you have the facility to use your computer in a very powerful way. You can use your computer as a system which stores information on the backing store in the form of files. This section is about the use of a particular kind of file called a *serial* or *sequential* file.

A file is defined as an organised series of records, where a record is a set of data relevant to, say, one person or item of stock. A good example of a file is a telephone directory where each record is a subscriber's name, address and telephone number. The records in a serial file are rather like a series of pieces of music stored on a reel of recording tape. On such a reel we have to wind past all the pieces preceding the one we are interested in, before we can reach the required item. Serial files can be held either on tape or discs, and for proper handling of files two cassette drives are desirable although only one disc drive is essential. Two disc drives are far better than one on its own. One very good reason for this is that two disc drives make it possible to copy from one disc to another, thus allowing duplication of the contents as an insurance against the possible destruction of the data on a disc, due to a failure of the drive mechanism. Because the data on a disc is read by a magnetic reading head, rather like a gramophone pickup, it is possible to read from one file and write to another, when both are held on the same disc. This is not possible without much rewinding when files are kept on tape.

Whatever version of BASIC you have available on your computer, there must be a series of program instructions for you to use in order to perform certain essential tasks associated with files. These are

(1) *Open a file* in order to have data written to it. This usually takes the form of an instruction which states the name you wish to give the file. Very often a number is allocated to the file, as well as a name. The name is a permanent name but the number is only used for reference during a program run. For example, a file may be called "SALES" but during the course of various programs which may use it, it may be referred to as File Number Ø, 1, 2, etc. Most systems allow more than one file to be open during the course of any program and the file number offers an easy way of referencing any particular file.

(2) *Open a file* in order to read data from it. This instruction will associate a unique number with a named file which already contains data. These data will have been written to by some other program.

(3) *Write data* to a file. Data which are written to a file one record at a time are written by means of a file writing instruction. After a record has been written to a file, the next file writing instruction will write data to the next record in sequence. Such an instruction will take the form of

"Write the current values of the variables A, B, N$, P$, Q to the next record of File No. 2"

(4) *Read data* from a file. Data are read from a file one record at a time and the data values read are assigned to specified variable names. Such an instruction will take the form of

"Read the data from the next record of File No. 3 and assign the values read to the variable names A, B, C$, D$, X".

In both this file statement and the previous one, the variable names must match the data types read, so that string values cannot be assigned to numeric names, and *vice versa*.

(5) *Detect the end of a file*. Empty records in a serial file contain what are called *end-of-file* markers, and when the last record has been read the next read instruction detects an empty record. The computer needs to be told what instruction to execute after detecting an end of file. If this is not done there will be an error message displayed and the program will come to a halt.

(6) *Close the file*. After a file has been used it is usually necessary to close it off. This is because a pointer keeps track of the records as they are read. The action of closing a file automatically resets the pointer to the beginning of the file, ready for the next time it is opened. This is important because a serial file can only exist in one mode at a time. A serial file has records stored in sequence just as an album of music on a tape cassette has the pieces stored in sequence. Any tape recording expert will tell you how difficult it is to replace one piece of music in the middle of a tape by another. What has to be done is to copy all the pieces up to the one to be changed on to another tape. Then the replacement piece is recorded in its appropriate place on the second tape. The rest of the pieces on the first tape can then be copied across on to the new tape. This needs two tape recorders, one with the original tape and set in playback mode. The second recorder will have the new, edited, tape on it and will be set in record mode. In computing we talk of files instead of albums and records within those files instead of music tracks. Instead of recordings and playback we talk of writing and reading. To sum up this concept it needs to be emphasised that:

(a) A serial file can, at one time, only be read from or written to.

(b) Because of the above a single record cannot be altered within a serial file.

The whole file, up to the record to be replaced, must be read across record by record to a new file. The record to be inserted is then placed in its proper place in sequence on the new file. Then the remaining records are read across to the new file.

(c) The new file can then be known by the name previously allocated to the old file and the old file either deleted or stored for archive purposes.

(7) *Delete a file*. When a file is opened it is said to be *created*, so that a completely empty file with a unique file name comes into existence on the backing store. When a file is of no further use it can be deleted from the backing store, very often with an instruction contained in a program. If this is not possible then a command to delete the file can be issued when the program has stopped.

(8) *Rename a file.* The name of a file can be changed by an instruction which states the name by which the file was previously known, and the new name by which it is to be known in future. The new name must be unique and not the name of any other file on the backing store. Such an instruction will take the form of

RENAME "GEORGE", "PHYLLIS"

where the first name is the original name, and the second name is the new name. Again, some versions of BASIC allow renaming to be done in a program while others insist that renaming is a separate command issued after a program has been run.

This activity does not attempt to illustrate anything more than two aspects of serial file handling and the use of the eight file instructions listed previously. The two examples have been written in a number of different versions of BASIC to illustrate the use of the varying sets of instructions used by different dialects of BASIC.

The first program illustrates the creation of a serial file, the writing of records to it, and the reading back of those records and their display on the screen. The second program illustrates the programming required to amend one record in a serial file. The steps involved in the two programs are written in simple English first.

Program 1

(1) Open a file called "FILE 1" for writing
(2) Type in two numbers and a name
(3) If the first of the numbers is zero go to step 6
(4) Write the two numbers and the name to the next record in sequence on the file
(5) Go to step 2

(6) Close the file
(7) Open the file called "FILE 1" for reading
(8) Read two numbers and a name from the next record in sequence from the file
(9) If an end-of-file marker is detected go to step 12
(10) Display the two numbers and the name on the screen
(11) Go to step 8
(12) Close the file
(13) Stop

Program 2

(1) Open a file called "FILE 1" for reading
(2) Open a file called "TEMPY" for writing
(3) Request the number of the record to be amended
(4) Read each record up to the one before the one to be amended from "FILE 1" to "TEMPY"
(5) Read the next record in "FILE 1" and display it on the screen
(6) Request the new data to be typed in
(7) Write the new data into the next record of "TEMPY"
(8) Read the data remaining on the file "FILE 1" one record at a time on to the file "TEMPY". When an end-of-file marker is detected close both files
(9) Open the file called "TEMPY" for reading
(10) Read the contents of the file "TEMPY" one record at a time and display the records on the screen. When an end-of-file marker is detected close the file
(11) Delete the file called "FILE 1"
(12) Rename the file "TEMPY", "FILE 1"

Notes on the programs

Activities 15.1a and 15.2a are written in Texas Instruments Super BASIC. Note that the end-of-file test comes before the reading instruction. It is saying, 'If the next thing you read is an end-of-file marker . . .'

Activities 15.1b and 15.2b are written in Research Machines 9K BASIC. In this version of the language no end-of-file marker is used. This is because the facility is only available if there is one data item per record. Because of this, another device is used to detect an end-of-file. A special value is placed in the last record, and it is this value which is tested for, to trigger off the end-of-file condition.

Activities 15.1c and 15.2c are written in Zilog BASIC which does not possess the ability to rename a file through a program statement. This has to be done as a separate command after the program has stopped.

```
10 OPEN "O",1,"B:FILE1"
20 INPUT X,Y,B$
30 IF X=0 THEN 60
40 PRINT#1,X,Y,B$
50 GOTO 20
60 CLOSE 1
70 OPEN "I",1,"B:FILE1"
80 IF EOF(1) THEN 120
90 INPUT#1,X,Y,B$
100 PRINT X,Y,B$
110 GOTO 80
120 CLOSE 1
130 END
```

Activity 15.1 (a)

```
10 OPEN "I",1,"B:FILE1"
20 OPEN "O",2,"B:TEMPY"
30 INPUT "WHICH RECORD DO YOU WISH TO AMEND ";N
40 FOR I=1 TO N-1
50 INPUT#1,X,Y,B$
60 PRINT#2,X,Y,B$
70 NEXT I
80 INPUT#1,X,Y,B$
90 PRINT X,Y,B$
100 INPUT "ENTER REPLACEMENT DATA ";X,Y,B$
110 PRINT#2,X,Y,B$
120 IF EOF(1) THEN 160
130 INPUT#1,X,Y,B$
140 PRINT#2,X,Y,B$
150 GOTO 120
160 CLOSE 1
170 CLOSE 2
180 OPEN "I",1,"B:TEMPY"
190 PRINT"THIS IS THE NEW FILE"
200 IF EOF(1) THEN 240
210 INPUT #1,X,Y,B$
220 PRINT X,Y,B$
230 GOTO 200
240 CLOSE 1
250 KILL"B:FILE1"
260 NAME "B:TEMPY" AS "B:FILE1"
270 END
```

Activity 15.2 (a)

```
10 CLEAR 20
20 FILES2,"FILE1"
30 INPUT X,Y,B$
40 IF X=0 THEN 70
50 PRINT#;X;",";Y;",";B$
60 GOTO 30
70 PRINT#;X;",";Y;",";"END"
75 FILES3
80 FILES 1,"FILE1"
90 INPUT#;X,Y,B$
100 IF B$="END" THEN 130
110 PRINT X,Y,B$
120 GOTO 90
130 STOP
```

Activity 15.1 (b)

```
10 CLEAR 20
20 FILES 1,"FILE1"
30 FILES 2,"TEMPY"
40 INPUT "WHAT RECORD DO YOU WISH TO AMEND ";N
50 FOR I=1 TO N-1
60 INPUT#;X,Y,B$
70 PRINT#;X;",";Y;",";B$
80 NEXT I
90 INPUT#;X,Y,B$
100 PRINT X,Y,B$
```

```
110 INPUT 'TYPE IN THE REPLACEMENT DATA';X,Y,B$
120 PRINT#;X;",";Y;",";B$
130 INPUT#;X,Y,B$
140 IN B$='END' THEN 170
150 PRINT#;X;",";Y;",";B$
160 GOTO 130
170 PRINT#;X;",";Y;",";B$
160 GOTO 130
170 PRINT#;X;",";Y;",";B$
180 PRINT'THIS IS THE NEW FILE'
190 FILES3
200 FILES 1,'TEMPY'
210 INPUT#;X;Y;B$
220 IF B$='END'THEN 250
230 PRINT X,Y,B$
240 GOTO 210
250 FILES 5,'FILE1'
260 FILES 6,'FILE1','TEMPY'
```

Activity 15.2 (b)

```
10 DIM B$(20),C$(20),D$(20)
15 LET C$='                    '\20 SPACES
20 FILE #1;'FILE1;ACC=IN;REC=36'
25 RESTORE #1
30 INPUT X,Y,B$
40 IF X=0 THEN 70
45 LET D$=C$+B$
50 WRITE #1;X,Y,B$
60 GOTO 30
70 CLOSE #1
80 FILE #1;'FILE1;ACC=IN;REC=36'
85 RESTORE #1
90 READ #1;X,Y,B$
100 IF EOF(1) THEN 140
110 PRINT X,Y,B$
120 GOTO 90
130 CLOSE #1
140 STOP
```

Activity 15.1 (c)

```
50 DIM B$(20),C$(20),D$(20)
60 LET C$='                    ' \20 SPACES
70 FILE #1;'FILE1;ACC=IN;REC=36'
80 FILE #2;'TEMPY;ACC=IN;REC=36'
90 INPUT'WHICH RECORD DO YOU WISH TO AMEND ? ',N
100 FOR I = 1 TO N-1
110 READ #1;X,Y,B$
120 WRITE #2;X,Y,B$
130 NEXT I
140 READ #1;X,Y,B$
150 PRINT X,Y,B$
160 INPUT 'TYPE IN THE REPLACEMENT DATA ',X,Y,B$
165 DET D$=B$+C$
170 WRITE #2;X,Y,D$
180 READ #1;X;Y;B$
190 IF EOF(1) THEN 210
200 GOTO 170
210 CLOSE #1,#2
220 PRINT 'THIS IS THE NEW FILE'
230 FILE #1;'TEMPY;ACC=IN;REC=36'
240 READ #1;X,Y,B$
250 IF EOF(1) THEN 280
260 PRINT X,Y,B$
270 GOTO 240
280 CLOSE #1
290 ERASE 'FILE1'
```

Activity 15.2 (c)

```
10 STRING=0
20 OPEN #1,FILE1
30 INPUT X,Y,B$
40 IF X=0 THEN 70
50 WRITE #1,X,Y,B$
60 GOTO 30
70 CLOSE #1
80 OPEN #1,FILE1
90 READ #1,X,Y,B$
100 IF EOF(1)=1 THEN 130
110 PRINT X,Y,B$
120 GOTO 90
130 CLOSE #1
```

Activity 15.1 (d)

```
10 STRING = 100
20 OPEN #1,FILE1
30 OPEN #2,TEMPY
40 INPUT "WHAT RECORD DO YOU WISH TO CHANGE ",K
50 FOR I = 1 TO K-1
60 READ #1,X,Y,B$
70 WRITE #2,X,Y,B$
80 NEXT I
90 READ #1,X,Y,B$
100 PRINT X,Y,B$
110 INPUT "TYPE IN REPLACEMENT DATA ",X,Y,B$
120 WRITE #2,X,Y,B$
130 READ #1,X,Y,B$
140 IF EOF(1)=1 THEN 180
150 WRITE #2,X,Y,B$
160 GOTO 130
170 CLOSE #1
180 CLOSE #2
190 OPEN #2,TEMPY
195 PRINT " THIS IS THE NEW FILE"
200 READ #2,X,Y,B$
210 IF EOF(2)=1 THEN 240
220 PRINT X,Y,B$
230 GOTO 200
240 CLOSE #2
250 KILL FILE1
260 RENAME TEMPY,FILE1
```

Activity 15.2 (d)

Activities 15.1d and 15.2d are written in Flex BASIC, and activities 15.1e and 15.2e are written in Alpha Micro BASIC. This example looks very different from the others as it is a rather refined version of the language which does not use line numbers, but instead it uses a concept common in other languages, that of labels attached to statements to which jumps have to be made.

Activities 15.1f and 15.2f are the same programs written in APPLESOFT BASIC using the currently latest available DOS (Disk Operating System). The major differences between these file commands and those used previously are twofold. One difference is that all files are handled by DOS and the file statements are handed over to DOS by prefixing them with the Control-D character. This is done by assigning the string character D$ the appropriate character, denoted by CHR$(4), which is then concatenated with the OPEN FILE1, WRITE FILE1, etc., commands. The other difference is that once a file has been opened and put into read or write mode then all input and output instructions move data between the computer and the disc and not between computer and keyboard or screen. This is why the whole of the file is read into the memory and then can be

```
! EXAMPLE PROGRAM NUMBER 1 WRITTEN FOR THE ALPHA MICRO COMPUTER

        OPEN £1,"FILE1.DAT",OUTPUT       ! OPEN FILE FOR OUTPUT
NEXTREC:                                 ! LABEL FOR NEXT RECORD
        INPUT "X   ",X                   ! GET VALUE OF X
        IF X=0 GOTO ENDINPUT             ! END IF X=0
        INPUT "Y   ";Y                   ! GET VALUE OF Y
        INPUT "B$ ";B$                   ! GET VALUE OF B$
        PRINT £1,X,Y,B$                  ! OUTPUT TO FILE
        GOTO NEXTREC                     ! GO FOR NEXT RECORD
ENDINPUT:                                ! LABEL FOR OUTPUT FILE CLOSING
        CLOSE £1                         ! CLOSE OUTPUT FILE
        OPEN £1,"FILE1.DAT",INPUT        ! OPEN FILE FOR INPUT
READNEXT:                                ! LABEL FOR GETTING NET RECORD FROM FILE
        INPUT £1,X,Y,B$                  ! GET NEXT RECORD FROM FILE
        IF EOF(1) GOTO FINISH            ! IF NO MORE GOTO FINISH
        PRINT X,Y,B$                     ! DISPLAY ON V.D.U.
        GOTO READNEXT                    ! GO TO GET NEXT RECORD FROM FILE
FINISH:                                  ! FINISH LABEL
        CLOSE £1                         ! CLOSE INPUT FILE
        END                              ! END PROGRAM
```

Activity 15.1 (e)

```
! EXAMPLE PROGRAM NUMBER 2 WRITTEN FOR THE ALPHA MICRO COMPUTER

        OPEN £1,"FILE1.DAT",INPUT                       ! OPEN INPUT FILE
        OPEN £2,"TEMPY.DAT",OUTPUT                      ! OPEN TEMPORARY FILE
        INPUT "WHICH RECORD DO YOU WISH TO AMEND ";N    ! GET RECORD NUMBER TO REPLACE
        FOR I=1 TO N-1                                  ! SEARCH FOR RECORD
        INPUT £1,X,Y,B$
        PRINT £2,X,Y,B$
        NEXT I
        INPUT £1,X,Y,B$                                 ! READ RECORD TO BE REPLACED
        PRINT X,Y,B$                                    ! DISPLAY IT ON VDU
        INPUT "ENTER REPLACEMENT DATA ";X,Y,B$          ! GET NEW DATA
NEXT'OUTREC:                                            ! LABEL TO READ REST OF FILE
        PRINT £2,X,Y,B$                                 ! WRITE DATA TO TEMPOTARY FILE
        INPUT £1,X,Y,B$                                 ! GET REST OF INPUT RECORDS
        IF EOF(1) GOTO FINISH                           ! TEST FO END OF INPUT FILE
        GOTO NEXT'OUTREC
FINISH:                                                 ! LABEL FOR END OF INPUT FILE
        CLOSE £1                                        ! CLOSE BOTH FILES
        CLOSE £2
        PRINT "THIS IS THE NEW FILE"                    ! DISPLAY MESSAGE ON VDU
        OPEN £2,"TEMPY.DAT",INPUT                       ! OPEN TEMPORARY FILE TO READ
NEXT'INPUTREC:                                          ! LABEL TO GET NEXT INPUT RECORD
        INPUT £2,X,Y,B$                                 ! READ NEXT INPUT RECORD
        IF EOF(2) GOTO CLOSING                          ! TEST FOR END OF FILE
        PRINT X,Y,B$                                    ! DISPLAY ON VDU IF NOT
        GOTO NEXT'INPUTREC                              ! AND GO FOR NEXT RECORD
CLOSING:                                                ! LABEL FOR CLOSE DOWN
        CLOSE £2                                        ! CLOSE TEMPORARY FILE
        KILL "FILE1.DAT"                                ! DELETE OLD FILE
        XCALL RENAME,"TEMPY.DAT","FILE1.DAT"            ! RENAME NEW FILE
        END                                             ! FINISHED
```

Activity 15.2 (e)

manipulated before being written back to the disc. In fact, if a file has been opened for WRITEing, all PRINTs cause data to be written to the disc and the inclusion of an INPUT instruction before the file is closed will cancel the WRITE command and can cause errors from which the program may not be able to recover. There are going to be a number of ways out of the problems this creates, but they will require a detailed knowledge of the particular system before being used.

All the previous programs are written to handle serial files on discs. Activities 15.1g and 15.2g are written to handle the same files, but on cassette tape, and so

```
10 D$=CHR$(4)
20 DIM B$(100),X(100),Y(100)
30 I=1
40 ONERR GOTO 100
50 PRINT D$;"OPEN FILE1"
60 PRINT D$;"READ FILE1"
70 INPUT X(I),Y(I),B$(I)
80 I=I+1
90 GOTO 70
100 PRINT D$;"CLOSE FILE1"
110 INPUT"WHICH RECORD DO YOU WISH TO AMEND ?";N
120 PRINT X(N),Y(N),B$(N)
130 INPUT"TYPE IN THE REPLACEMENT DATA ";X(N),Y(N),B$(N)
140 PRINT "THIS IS THE NEW FILE"
150 FOR J=1 TO I-1
160 PRINT X(J),Y(J),B$(J)
170 NEXT J
180 PRINT D$;"OPEN TEMPY"
190 PRINT D$;"WRITE TEMPY"
200 FOR J=1 TO I-1
210 PRINT X(J),Y(J),B$(J)
220 NEXT J
230 PRINT D$;"CLOSE TEMPY"
240 PRINT D$;"DELETE FILE1"
250 PRINT D$;"RENAME TEMPY,FILE1"
```

Activity 15.1 (f)

```
10 D$=CHR$(4)
20 DIM B$(100),X(100),Y(100)
30 I=1
40 INPUT X(I),Y(I),B$(I)
50 IF X(I)=0 THEN 80
60 I=I+1
70 GOTO 40
80 I=I-1
90 PRINT D$;"OPEN FILE1"
100 PRINT D$;"WRITE FILE1"
110 FOR J=1 TO I
120 PRINT X(J),Y(J),B$(J)
130 NEXT J
140 PRINT D$;"CLOSE FILE1"
150 PRINT D$;"OPEN FILE1"
160 PRINT D$;"READ FILE1"
170 FOR J=1 TO I
180 INPUT X(J),Y(J),B$(J)
190 NEXT J
200 PRINT D$;"CLOSE FILE1"
210 FOR J=1 TO I
220 PRINT X(J),Y(J),B$(J)
230 NEXT J
```

Activity 15.2 (f)

```
10 OPEN 1,1,1,"FILE1"
20 INPUT X,Y,B$
25 IF X=0 THEN 80
30 PRINT#1,X;",";Y;",";B$
40 GOTO 20
80 CLOSE 1
90 PRINT "TO PRINT THE CONTENTS OF THE FILE"
100 PRINT "CREATED BY THIS PROGRAM RUN THE PROGRAM CALLED 'PRINT'"
110 PRINT "TO AMEND THE FILE CREATED BY THIS PROGRAM RUN 'UPDATE'"
```

```
10 INPUT "FILENAME ";N$
15 OPEN 1,1,0,N$
20 INPUT#1,X,Y,B$
30 IF ST=0 THEN PRINT X,Y,B$
40 IF ST=64 THEN 80
50 GOTO 20
80 PRINT X,Y,B$
90 CLOSE 1
100 PRINT "TO AMEND THIS FILE RUN THE PROGRAM 'UPDATE'"
```

Activity 15.1 (g)

the programs, and the way they are used, have to be modified. The programs are written in CBM BASIC.

Activity 15.1g consists now of two programs called "INPUT" and "PRINT" and for the purpose of this example the file, called "FILE 1", is written on to the cassette loaded on to cassette drive 1. First of all the "INPUT" program creates the file, and the data are written to it. The tape then has to be rewound by the user so that the reading of the tape can commence at the start of the file when the program called "PRINT" is run. This successfully completes the first programming activity.

For activity 15.2g to be completed, programs called "UPDATE" and "RENAME" are used in conjunction with the "PRINT" program.

The program called "UPDATE" copies all the file data, with the exception of the data which are required to be updated, from "FILE 1" on drive 1, on to a

```
10 OPEN 1,1,0,"FILE1"
20 OPEN 2,2,1,"TEMPY"
30 INPUT"WHICH RECORD DO YOU WISH TO AMEND ";N
40 FOR I = 1 TO N-1
50 INPUT#1,X,Y,B$
60 PRINT#2,X;",";Y;",";B$
70 NEXT I
80 INPUT#1,X,Y,B$
90 PRINT X,Y,B$
100 INPUT"TYPE IN NEW DATA";X,Y,B$
110 PRINT#2,X;",";Y;",";B$
120 INPUT#1,X,Y,B$
125 IF ST=0 THEN PRINT#2,X;",";Y;",";B$
130 IF ST=64 THEN 160
150 GOTO 120
160 PRINT#2,X;",";Y;",";B$
170 CLOSE 1
180 CLOSE 2
190 PRINT "TO RENAME THE NEW WITH THE ORIGINAL FILENAME RUN 'RENAME'"
200 PRINT "TO PRINT THE CONTENTS OF THE NEW FILE RUN 'PRINT'"
```

```
10 PRINT "IN ORDER TO USE THIS PROGRAM THE"
20 PRINT "FILE TO BE RENAMED MUST BE LOADED"
30 PRINT "IN CASSETTE DRIVE #2"
40 PRINT "A BLANK CASSETTE TO TAKE THE RENAMED
50 PRINT "FILE SHOULD BE IN DRIVE #1"
60 INPUT "O.K. ";A$
70 IF A$="YES" THEN 90
80 GOTO 10
90 INPUT "OLD FILE NAME ";O$
100 INPUT "NEW FILE NAME ";N$
110 OPEN 1,2,0,O$
120 OPEN 2,1,1,N$
130 INPUT#1,X,Y,B$
140 IF ST=0 THEN PRINT#2,X;",";Y;",";B$
150 IF ST=64 THEN 170
160 GOTO 130
170 PRINT#2,X;",";Y;",";B$
180 CLOSE 1
190 CLOSE 2
200 PRINT "RUN PROGRAM 'PRINT' TO CHECK
210 PRINT "THE CONTENTS OF THE NEW FILE"
```

Activity 15.2 (g)

new file called "TEMPY" which is in the cassette drive number 2. The data to be updated are entered from the keyboard as with all the other versions. At the end of "UPDATE" the tape has to be rewound, and the program called "PRINT" will print the data now on the new file. Finally, "TEMPY" is rewound again, and the program called "RENAME" is used to copy all the contents of the file "TEMPY" across to a new file called "FILE 1", which is on drive 1. This can either overwrite the existing data on the old tape which held "FILE 1", or have the file written on to a blank tape. If the latter method is used then an archival system of files can be set up, so that out-of-date information is not destroyed. It may often be useful to preserve a number of 'generations' of a file in case disaster strikes.

The program "RENAME" has to be used with tape files since, when a file is created, there is always a *header block* written at the start of the tape containing, among other things, the name of the file. This header block cannot be changed without changing the rest of the file.

If nothing else, this activity shows one advantage that discs have over tape.

Activity 16

General

This is an activity for you to browse through. It contains a number of programs which use features covered in all the previous activities, and includes illustrated games, a simulation and a teaching program. The object of these programs is to illustrate the wide range which can be written using the BASIC instructions covered in this book. Very often it is found that programs written by other people never quite do what we require them to do, and this activity attempts to demonstrate the types which can be put together from what is really a fairly limited set of instructions. It is very easy then to amend the programs to introduce features which suit your particular purpose.

```
30 DIM X(3)
40 PRINT
50 PRINT
60 PRINT
70 PRINT
80 PRINT"WELCOME TO THE CASINO!"
100 N=RND(1)
110 S=0
120 PRINT
130 PRINT "HOW MUCH DO YOU WANT TO BET ";
140 INPUT B
150 IF B= INT(B) THEN 190
160 PRINT
170 PRINT" YOU CAN ONLY BET EVEN MONEY"
180 GOTO 120
190 IF B<1001 THEN 220
200 PRINT"THAT'S TOO MUCH MONEY"
210 GOTO 120
220 IF B>0 THEN 250
230 PRINT"COME ON - LET'S GET DOWN TO BUSINESS!"
240 GOTO 120
250 PRINT
260 PRINT"VERY GOOD - AFTER EACH PULL I WILL ASK IF YOU WANT TO ";
270 PRINT"GO AGAIN. IF DO, TYPE 'P'. IF NOT TYPE ";
280 PRINT"'Q' FOR QUIT"
290 GOTO 370
300 PRINT
310 PRINT"AGAIN"
320 INPUT A$
330 IF A$="Q" THEN 1040
340 IF A$ ="P" THEN 370
350 PRINT"WHAT";
360 GOTO 320
370 PRINT
380 FOR I= 1 TO 3
390 X(I)=INT(RND(1)*8)+1
400 IF X(I)>5 THEN 600
410 IF X(I)>2 THEN 490
420 IF X(I)=2 THEN 460
430 PRINT"CHERRY ";
440 X(I)=1
450 GOTO 730
```

```
460 PRINT"ORANGE ";
470 X(I)=2
480 GOTO 730
490 IF X(I)>3 THEN 530
500 PRINT"LEMON ";
510 X(I)=3
520 GOTO 730
530 IF X(I)=5 THEN 570
540 PRINT"PLUM ";
550 X(I)=4
560 GOTO 730
570 PRINT"BELL ";
580 X(I)=5
590 GOTO 730
600 IF X(I)>7 THEN 690
610 IF X(I)=7 THEN 670
620 IF I<>1 THEN 640
630 IF RND(1)<0.8 THEN 460
640 PRINT"BAR    ";
650 X(I)=6
660 GOTO 730
670 IF I=2 THEN 430
680 GOTO 500
690 IF I=1 THEN 570
700 IF I<>3 THEN 720
710 IF X(1)<6 THEN 640
720 GOTO 540
730 NEXT I
740 P=0
750 IF X(1)>1 THEN 770
760 P=2
770 IF X(1)=X(2) THEN 830
780 IF P>0 THEN 990
790 S=S-B
800 PRINT"YOU LOSE !!"
810 PRINT"TOTAL = ";S
820 GOTO 300
830 IF X(2)=X(3) THEN 880
840 IF X(1)=1 THEN 860
850 IF X(3)<6 THEN 790
860 P=5
870 GOTO 990
880 IF X(1)=1 THEN 860
890 IF X(1)>2 THEN 920
900 P=8
910 GOTO 990
920 IF X(1)>4 THEN 950
930 P=12
940 GOTO 990
950 IF X(1)>5 THEN 980
960 P=20
990 W=P*B
1000 S=S+W-B
1010 PRINT"YOU WIN !!!"
1020 PRINT" TOTAL = ";S
1030 GOTO 300
1040 IF S<1000 THEN 1080
1050 PRINT"WE ARE HAPPY TO SEE YOU LEAVE,";
1060 PRINT" WE HATE TO LOSE THAT MUCH CASH!!"
1070 STOP
1080 IF S>0 THEN 1110
1090 PRINT"COME AGAIN!! WE LIKE YOUR MONEY"
1100 STOP
1110 PRINT"O.K. - YOU WON - BUT NOT A LOT!!"
1120 STOP
READY.
```

Activity 16.1

Activity 16.1 simulates the action of a 'one-armed bandit' slot-machine and activity 16.2 is the game of 'hangman', which is a word-guessing game. You can easily amend the DATA lines at the end of the program to include words of your own choosing. The program in activity 16.3 is one which can be used to help in the teaching of the rules for the addition of two fractions. It starts off with simple addition sums and, as the session progresses, the sums become more and

```
30 C=0
40 Y=0
50 PRINT"DO YOU KNOW THE RULES ";
60 INPUT Y$
70 IF Y$="YES" THEN 140
80 PRINT"THE COMPUTER PICKS A WORD"
90 PRINT"AND YOU HAVE 11 GUESSES TO FIND IT."
100 PRINT"AT ANY TIME YOU MAY GUESS A LETTER OR"
110 PRINT"A WORD"
130 PRINT"REMEMBER THAT A SPACE IS A CHARACTER"
140 M=INT(RND(1)*80)+1
150 FOR N = 1 TO M
160 READ C$
170 NEXT N
180 L=LEN(C$)
190 H=11
200 P$=""
210 FOR N = 1 TO L
220 G$=P$+"-"
230 P$=G$
240 NEXT N
250 PRINT
260 PRINT"O.K. - I'VE CHOSEN A WORD"
265 PRINT"IT IS ";L;" LETTERS LONG"
270 PRINT
280 PRINTTAB(20);P$;TAB(22+L);"YOU HAVE 11 GUESSES"
290 PRINT
300 INPUT"YOUR GUESS IS ";Y$
310 IF LEN(Y$)=1 THEN 340
320 IF Y$=C$ THEN 490
330 GOTO 420
340 REM
350 FOR N=1 TO L
360 IF LEFT$(Y$,1)<>MID$(C$,N,1) THEN 390
370 G$=LEFT$(P$,N-1)+MID$(C$,N,1)+RIGHT$(P$,L-N)
380 P$=G$
390 NEXT N
400 IF P$=C$ THEN 490
410 GOTO 430
420 PRINT"HARD LUCK !"
430 H=H-1
440 PRINT TAB(20);P$
445 PRINT"YOU HAVE ";H;" GUESSES LEFT"
446 PRINT
450 IF H>0 THEN 300
460 C=C+1
470 PRINT"I'M SORRY - YOU LOST. THAT'S ";C;" TO ME"
475 PRINT
480 GOTO 525
490 Y=Y+1
500 PRINT
520 PRINT"WELL DONE. THAT'S ";Y;" TO YOU"
525 PRINT"THE WORD WAS ";C$
526 PRINT
527 PRINT
528 RESTORE
530 PRINT"DO YOU WANT ANOTHER GAME ";
535 INPUT Y$
540 IF Y$="YES" THEN 140
550 PRINT"BYE"
560 STOP
570 DATA ABBOT,ABLAZE,ALKALI,ALCHEMY,ASYMPTOTE,ASPHALT
580 DATA BEGUILE,BELLICOSE,BRADAWL,BRASIER,CARNIVAL
590 DATA CASCADE,CLASP,CLING,CONFIRM,CONGEAL,DANK
600 DATA DEBT,DIMPLE,DIRGE,DRENCH,DRIZZLE,ENRAGE
610 DATA ENTHUSIASTIC,FALSE,FAHRENHEIT,FLUID,FLY
620 DATA GAZELLE,GIBBERISH,HANDCUFF,HALVE,HOWITZER
630 DATA INCREMENT,INEDIBLE,INVOICE,INK,KNACK
640 DATA JURY,LAWYER,LATHE
650 DATA OSTLER,OUST,PEEK,PERCH,POKE,POLYTECHNIC
660 DATA PRIVILEGE,PROPEL,QUAY,RATIFY,RETRACE,RETCH
670 DATA SAVANNA,SCALDING,SHERIFF,SHAM,SNIP,SOLITARY,SNUG
680 DATA SWAMP,SURGE,THRASH,TILT,TWIST,TYPICAL
690 DATA UNIMPEACHABLE,UNIQUE,VAGRANT,VARIATION
700 DATA WHIPPERSNAPPER,WHET,XYLOPHONE,ZENITH
710 DATA DIATHERMACY,DINGBAT,WALLABY,WALLOON
720 DATA PRECIOUS,CUTE,DIABOLICAL
730 END
```

Activity 16.2

more difficult. The program checks the answer supplied by the user, and if three incorrect answers are given, gives the answer and sets a new sum. Finally activity 16.4 is a simple statistics program which will calculate the mean and standard deviation of a set of data points. It will then test the data for an approximation to a normal distribution. This data is stored in a set of DATA lines at the end of

```
20 PRINT" THIS PROGRAM WILL HELP YOU TO ADD FRACTIONS TOGETHER"
30 A5=1
40 PRINT" YOU SHOULD KNOW THE MEANING OF THE WORD 'NUMERATOR'
50 PRINT" AND WHAT L.C.M. STANDS FOR"
60 PRINT
70 H=1
80 PRINT
90 PRINT" HERE WE GO !"
95 PRINT
100 INPUT"WHAT IS YOUR NAME ";N$
110 DIM A(50),B(50),C(50),L(50),N(50),M(50)
120 REM**PLACE THE APPROPRIATE CLEAR SCREEN CHARACTER HERE**
130 LET A=RND(-T1)
140 A5=A5+1
150 E1=0
160 E2=0
170 IF A5>11 THEN LET A5=11
180 A=INT(RND(1)*A5+1)
190 GOSUB 1940
200 B=R
210 GOSUB 1940
220 C=R
230 GOSUB 1940
240 D=R
250 IF A>= B THEN 180
260 IF C>=D THEN 210
270 A1=A
280 B1=B
290 GOSUB 1790
300 IF X1=1 THEN 340
310 A=A/X1
320 B=B/X1
330 GOTO 270
340 A1=C
350 B1=D
360 GOSUB 1790
370 IF X1=1 THEN 410
380 C=C/X1
390 D=D/X1
400 GOTO 340
410 IF A5=2 THEN 430
420 IF A/B =C/D THEN 180
425 REM**PLACE THE APPROPRIATE CLEAR SCREEN CHARACTER HERE**
430 PRINT" THIS IS YOUR SUM"
440 PRINT
450 PRINT TAB(10);A;TAB(14);C
460 PRINT TAB(11);"-";" + ";"-"
470 PRINT TAB(10);B;TAB(14);D
480 GOSUB 1150
490 INPUT" WHAT IS THE L.C.M ";P1
500 IF P=P1 THEN 580
510 IF P1/P=INT(P1/P) THEN 530
520 GOTO 540
530 PRINT"THAT'S O.K. - BUT IT'S NOT THE LOWEST COMMON MULTIPLE"
540 E1=E1+1
550 IF E1>3 THEN 590
560 PRINT"TRY AGAIN ";N$
570 GOTO 490
580 PRINT" RIGHT YOU ARE -";
590 PRINT"THE L.C.M. IS ";P
600 N1=A*P/B+C*P/D
610 INPUT"WHAT IS THE NUMERATOR ";N2
620 IF N1=N2 THEN 670
630 E2=E2+1
640 IF E2>3 THEN 680
650 PRINT"TRY AGAIN ";N$
660 GOTO 610
670 PRINT"GOOD - ";
680 PRINT" THE NUMERATOR IS ";N1
690 GOSUB 1970
700 PRINT
```

```
710 A1=N1
720 B1=P
730 GOSUB 1790
740 IF X1=1 THEN 780
750 N1=N1/X1
760 P=P/X1
770 GOTO 710
780 PRINT"ANSWER:-"
790 PRINT
800 IF N1<=P THEN 990
810 H=0
820 GOTO 990
830 PRINT "CAN WE SIMPLIFY THIS ANSWER ";N$;
840 H=1
850 INPUT A$
860 IF A$="YES" THEN 900
870 E2=E2+1
880 PRINT"BUT ISN'T THIS FRACTION TOP HEAVY ?"
890 PRINT"WHY NOT ";
900 PRINT"DIVIDE IT OUT AND YOU SHOULD GET:-"
910 M1=N1-INT(N1/P)*P
920 IF M1<>0 THEN 950
930 PRINT INT(N1/P)
940 GOTO 1070
950 PRINT TAB(10);M1
960 PRINT TAB(8);INT(N1/P);"-"
970 PRINTTAB(10);P
980 GOTO 1070
990 PRINT TAB(10);N1
1000 PRINT TAB(11);"--"
1010 PRINT TAB(10);P
1020 PRINT
1030 PRINT
1040 IF N1=P THEN PRINT"THE ANSWER IS ";INT(N1/P)
1050 IF N1=P THEN 1070
1060 IF H=0 THEN 830
1070 PRINT"YOU MADE ";E1+E2;"ERRORS ";N$
1080 IF E1+E2<>0 THEN 1100
1090 PRINT"GOOD FOR YOU !"
1100 PRINT" DO YOU WANT TO TRY ANOTHER ";
1110 INPUT A$
1120 IF A$="YES" THEN 130
1121 REM**PLACE THE APPROPRIATE CLEAR SCREEN CHARACTER HERE**
1130 PRINT"HOPE YOU LEARNED SOMETHING FROM THIS ";N$
1131 PRINT "GOODBYE"
1133 STOP
1140 REM***CALCULATION OF L.C.M.S***
1150 N=B
1160 GOSUB 1260
1170 FOR K=1 TO I-1
1180 N(K)=A(K)
1190 NEXT K
1200 N=D
1210 GOSUB 1260
1220 FOR J=1 TO I-1
1230 M(J)=A(J)
1240 NEXT J
1250 GOTO 1370
1260 I=1
1270 IF N=1 THEN 1360
1280 FOR F=INT(N/2) TO 1 STEP -1
1290 IF N/F<> INT(N/F) THEN 1330
1300 A(I)=N/F
1310 I=I+1
1320 GOTO 1340
1330 NEXT F
1340 N=F
1350 GOTO 1270
1360 RETURN
1370 IF K>J THEN 1480
1380 FOR Z=1 TO J-1
1390 B(Z)=M(Z)
1400 NEXT Z
1410 FOR Z=1 TO K-1
1420 C(Z)=N(Z)
1430 NEXT Z
1440 S=K-1
1450 L=J-1
1460 P=L
1470 GOTO 1570
1480 FOR Z=1 TO K-1
```

```
1490 B(Z)=N(Z)
1500 NEXT Z
1510 FOR Z=1 TO J-1
1520 C(Z)=M(Z)
1530 NEXT Z
1540 S=J-1
1550 L=K-1
1560 P=L
1570 FOR Z=1 TO L
1580 L(Z)=B(Z)
1590 NEXT Z
1600 I=0
1610 I=I+1
1620 Z=1
1630 IF C(I)=B(Z) THEN 1670
1640 IF Z=P THEN 1740
1650 Z=Z+1
1660 GOTO 1630
1670 B(Z)=-1
1680 IF I<>S THEN 1610
1690 P=1
1700 FOR I=1 TO L
1710 P=P*L(I)
1720 NEXT I
1730 GOTO 1770
1740 L=L+1
1750 L(L)=C(I)
1760 GOTO 1680
1770 RETURN
1780 REM**CALC OF H.C.F.S**
1790 IF A1>B1 THEN 1820
1800 X1=B1
1810 GOTO 1830
1820 X1=A1
1830 IF A1<B1 THEN1860
1840 X2=B1
1850 GOTO 1870
1860 X2=A1
1870 X3=X2
1880 X2=(X2*(X1/X2-INT(X1/X2)))
1890 X2=X2+.5
1900 X2=INT(X2)
1910 X1=X3
1920 IF X2<>0 THEN1870
1930 RETURN
1940 REM**SUBROUTINE FOR GENERATION OF INTEGERS**
1950 R=INT(RND(1)*A5+1)
1960 RETURN
1970 IF N1<>P THEN RETURN
1980 PRINT"THIS GIVES US -"
1990 PRINT TAB(10);N1
2000 PRINT TAB(11);"---"
2010 PRINT TAB(10);P
2020 PRINT"WHICH CANCELS DOWN TO GIVE US :-"
2030 RETURN
```

Activity 16.3

the program. Activity 16.4a shows the changes made to the program to enable the data to be read from a file stored on a cassette. If these changes are made to the program, and the DATA lines deleted, the program then becomes far more useful.

```
READY.

 20 DIM G(100),F(100)
 30 N=100
 40 K=1
 50 INPUT"CELL SIZE = ";I1
 60 INPUT"LOWEST VALUE = ";L
 70 F=0
 80 READ G(K)
 90 IF G(K)=9999 THEN 140
 100 S1=S1+G(K)
 110 S=S+(G(K)^2)
 120 K=K+1
 130 GOTO 80
```

```
140 N1=K-1
150 D=SQR((S-S1^2/N1)/(N1-1))
160 S1=S1/N1
170 K=0
180 FOR I=2 TO N1
190 IF G(I-1)<=G(I) THEN 240
200 K=G(I-1)
210 G(I-1)=G(I)
220 G(I)=K
230 K=1
240 NEXT I
250 IF K THEN 170
260 IF 2*INT(N1/2)<>N1 THEN 290
270 P=(G(N1/2)+G(N1/2+1))/2
280 GOTO 300
290 P=G(INT(N1/2+1))
300 FOR H=1 TO N
310 G(H)=0
320 NEXT H
330 RESTORE
340 FOR K=1 TO N1
350 READ D1
360 D1=INT(((D1-L)/I1)+.0001)+1
370 G(D1)=G(D1)+1
380 NEXT K
390 FOR K=1 TO N
400 IF G(K)=0 THEN 420
410 M=K
420 NEXT K
430 M1=0
440 FOR K =1 TO M
450 IF G(K)<=M1 THEN 470
460 M1=G(K)
470 NEXT K
480 PRINT N1;" DATA POINTS"
485 PRINT "CELL SIZE = ";I1
490 PRINT TAB(5);"MEAN = ";S1
495 PRINT TAB(5);"MEDIAN = ";P
500 PRINT TAB(5);"STANDARD DEVIATION = ";D
510 PRINT TAB(6);"MAXIMUM FREQUENCY = ";M1
520 INPUT"DO YOU WISH TO TEST FOR NORMALITY ";A$
530 IF A$ = "YES" THEN 560
540 IF A$ = "NO" THEN STOP
550 GOTO 520
560 DEF FNF(X)=.39894*(EXP(-.5*X^2))
570 A=-6
580 E=.001
590 PRINT TAB(15);"THEORETICAL","OBSERVED"
600 PRINT"MID POINT","        FREQUENCY","FREQUENCY"
610 FOR I =1 TO M-1
620 B=((L+I*I1)-S1)/D
630 H=(B-A)/2
640 T=(FNF(A)+FNF(B))*H
650 I2=3*T
660 N=1
670 G=0
680 FOR K=1 TO N
690 G=G+FNF(A+(2*K-1)*H)
700 NEXT K
710 I3=T+4*H*G
720 IF ABS(I3-I2)<3*E THEN 780
730 N=2*N
740 T=(T+I3)/4
750 I2=I3
760 H=H/2
770 GOTO 670
780 F(I)=I3/3*N1
790 PRINT L+(I-.5)*I1,F(I),G(I)
800 C=C+((G(I)-F(I))^2)/F(I)
810 A=B
820 Z=Z+F(I)
830 NEXT I
840 F(M)=N1-Z
850 PRINT L+(M+.5)*I1,F(M),G(M)
860 PRINT "CALCULATED VALUE OF CHI SQUARED IS ";C;
870 PRINT" WITH ";M-3;" DEGREES OF FREEDOM"
880 STOP
890 DATA 8,5,2,3,6,9,5,4,2,5,7,5,3
900 DATA 5,2,3,6,9,5,1,2,4,7,8,5,6,6
910 DATA 12,15,14,11,12,15,14,10,13,17
920 DATA 16,12,13,14,10,17,18,19,18,17,9999
READY.
```

Activity 16.4

```
72 INPUT "FILENAME ";N$
74 OPEN 1,1,0,N$
76 INPUT#1,Q
78 IF ST=0 THEN G(K)=Q
80 IF ST=64 THEN 140
100 S1=S1+G(K)
110 S=S+(G(K)^2)
120 K=K+1
130 GOTO 76
140 CLOSE 1
141 PRINT"REWIND TAPE NOW"
142 N1=K
```

```
330 OPEN 1,1,0,N$
340 FOR K=1 TO N1
350 INPUT#1,D1
360 D1=INT(((D1-L)/I1)+.0001)+1
370 G(D1)=G(D1)+1
380 NEXT K
385 CLOSE 1
```

Activity 16.4 (a)

The remaining chapters of this book should give you some help in obtaining the best from your microcomputer system, whatever its make, and whatever the facilities it provides.

BASIC commands

As well as the program instructions mentioned in the various activities, BASIC possesses a comprehensive set of commands. A command is an instruction which can exist outside the program, and is applied to the current program stored in RAM. For example, the command RUN is probably the most commonly used command, and is really an instruction to the BASIC interpreter to go to the lowest numbered line in the program, interpret it, and then execute it. RUN 1ØØ is the command for the program to begin executing at line 100.

LIST is the command to copy the current program in RAM, line by line, on to the video screen. A command such as LLIST, or possibly PLIST, is a command to output the program, line by line, on to a printer, should one be part of your system. Every system with a printer will have such a command available.

SAVE is the command which will place a copy of the program currently in RAM on to the backing store. The program saved must, however, be uniquely identified by a name, and so the SAVE command must be followed by the name you give the program, so that it can be recalled from backing store, tape or disc, at some future time.

```
SAVE "B.TEST"
```

is a typical command for the current program to be stored away on drive B under the name of "TEST". Not all disc-based systems have identical sets of commands, but they must all have commands equivalent to this.

After a program has been SAVEd it can be retrieved from backing store by a command such as

```
LOAD"PROGRAM"
```

by which the program named "PROGRAM" is copied from the backing store and loaded into RAM ready for running. If a program is on any disc which is not the main drive, usually called Drive 1 or Drive A, then a command such as

```
LOAD"B.TEST"
```

will cause the program called "TEST" to be loaded into RAM from Drive B. If the drive is unspecified then BASIC assumes that the main drive is meant. The BASIC interpreter is always located on the main drive.

The NEW command is the command which erases the current program from RAM and leaves the way open for new programs to be written. NEW is always used after one program has been written, tested and saved. The command LOAD always causes an automatic NEW to be done, prior to the entry of a fresh program from the backing store.

When a program is being written, it is not uncommon for extra lines to be inserted between existing lines. It is for this reason that we usually number programs in increments of 10. If a program ends up with lines numbered in a haphazard manner then RENUMBER will cause them to be renumbered in increments of 10, and with the first line being given the line number 10. The renumbering procedure automatically takes into account the GOTOs, the IF . . .THENs and all other types of jumps, and renumbers them accordingly. If required, renumbering can take place in increments other than 10. For example

```
RENUMBER 1Ø, 5
```

would mean that the renumbering should be in increments of 5, with 10 being the number of the first line.

Although the operating system, which is covered in a later chapter, is the main tool for handling files on disc, BASIC does offer a number of facilities in that direction. There is always a command for getting rid of files from backing store, particularly useful if a program has been amended, and a better version is required to be put in place of an earlier version. The usual commands are KILL or DELETE. Another facility is that of renaming files and this will usually take the form of.

```
RENAME "OLDFILE", "NEWFILE"
```

where the first name is that of the file to be renamed and the second name is that by which it is to be known in future. The new name must not, of course, be that of any file already in existence.

Most versions of BASIC allow some of the commands to be used as part of the program as well as commands outside of the program structure. This means that the same instructions which can be used inside a program to delete and rename files can be used outside in order to delete and rename programs. This is shown in particular in the programs forming activity 15.

Bug - hunting, or why my programs never work first time

It is almost a law of nature that no program of more than four lines ever works first time. The reasons for this are manifold but they can be put down in many cases, to very simple errors of typing, or to the use of the BASIC language itself. Errors in computer programs are usually called *bugs*, and the various ways of debugging a program form the basis of this chapter. An attempt is made to itemise the various types of error, but it is often a combination of several of these which causes a program to fail.

(1) *Typing errors*

These errors are sometimes difficult to spot since it is a human failing to see what we want to see, particularly when checking a program listing. We strike the wrong key and produce an error which fools us, and the BASIC interpreter as well. For example, one program the author wrote failed consistently to work properly and eventually the error was tracked down to a line which should have read

```
215 LET T = 1Ø
```

having been mistyped as

```
215 LEY T = 1Ø
```

Now it is quite true to say that LEY is not a BASIC instruction, but unfortunately, the BASIC interpreter being used at the time allowed variable names to be longer than one letter, or one letter followed by a digit. Not only that, but the LET, as is usual, was optional and the value of 10 was allocated to a variable called LEY T, spaces being allowable in names as well, instead of to the variable T. The moral of this is to check program listings very carefully indeed. This, of course, is another powerful argument in favour of not using the word LET in an assignment statement. If the line had been written as

```
215 T = 1Ø
```

in the first place the problem would never have arisen.

(2) *Wrongly numbered lines*

An error caused by wrongly numbered lines is often difficult to track down. This is because the fault is shown up by an error message which says that a jump cannot be made to a line with a particular number, as that line does not exist. The problem then becomes one of finding to where the jump ought to have been made in the first place. A good way of detecting this type of error before the program is run is to issue the RENUMBER command. This will attempt to renumber the lines of the program, and any unresolved GOTO statements will cause an error message to be issued. Very often the BASIC interpreter will cause unresolved GOTO statements to be listed as GOTO ØØØØ. In this case the detective work has to start in order to find to where the jump should be made. Once the inconsistency has been sorted out the program can be test run.

(3) *Wrongly nested loops*

If one loop lies within another then it must lie wholly within it. If you refer to activity 12 you will find an example of this where we have

```
┌─FOR I = ......
│┌FOR J = ......
││
│└NEXT J
└─NEXT I
```

To have an arrangement such as

```
 ┌FOR I = ......
┌┼FOR J = ......
││
│└NEXT I
└─NEXT J
```

is illegal and will cause messages such as

NEXT WITHOUT FOR

or

FOR WITHOUT NEXT

to be output.

(4) *Hard loops*

At its worst this error is typified by a program statement such as

45 GOTO 45

This error is usually apparent if nothing happens when some form of output is expected. If this happens then it is often a good idea to stop the execution of a program; you may have a RUN STOP key, in which case the program will halt and the line at which the halt took place will be printed on the screen. CONT or CON will usually continue the program, and after this has been done a few times it is usually fairly clear what the program is doing and where it is looping. If you are in doubt about the path the program is taking then insert a few extra PRINT statements which indicate where the program is at any time. If the value of the relevant variables are printed at regular intervals then the result can be very revealing. Remember that some microcomputers do not perform some calculations very quickly and what appears to be a hard loop is, in fact, a perfectly correct, but lengthy, set of calculations. A good example of this is in the program listed in activity 16.4 where there is a section where the numbers are sorted into order. The sort used in that program is not particularly efficient if a large number of data items is sorted.

If the part of the program in doubt is, for example,

```
124Ø FOR I = 1 TO J – 1
125Ø LET M(I) = A(I)
126Ø NEXT I
```

as happened in the development of one of the programs used in this book, then an extra line was inserted which was

```
1255 PRINT "AT LINE 1255";M(I);A(I)
```

and the program rerun. Once the error was corrected the extra line, line 1255, was deleted and the program was found to be satisfactory.

(5) *Problems with FOR. . .NEXT. . . loops*

This type of error can be very frustrating to search for and is due to the fact that not all FOR. . .NEXT. . . loops work in the same way. The simple program shown below illustrates the point. Try it on your system and see the result.

```
1Ø INPUT A,B,C
2Ø FOR I = A TO B STEP C
3Ø PRINT I;
4Ø NEXT I
5Ø PRINT "EXIT VALUE OF I ";I
6Ø END
```

Use values of A,B,C of 1,10,1, then 1,1,1 and finally 5,1,1 and compare the results with the outputs shown in figure 23 where the results of running this program using different versions of BASIC are shown. The differences occur because of the different points in the loop where the index variable, I, is updated. Also note that it is possible to traverse a loop even though the target value is smaller than the initial value of I.

```
10   INPUT A,B,C
20   FOR I=A TO B STEP C
30     PRINT I;
40   NEXT I
50   PRINT "EXIT VALUE OF I IS ";I
60   END
RUN


?1,10,1
 1      2      3      4      5      6      7      8      9      10
EXIT VALUE OF I IS  11

DONE
RUN


?1,1,1
 1      EXIT VALUE OF I IS  2

DONE
RUN


?5,1,1
EXIT VALUE OF I IS  5

DONE
```

Figure 23 (a)

```
10 INPUT A,B,C
20 FOR I=A TO B STEP C
30 PRINT I;
40 NEXT I
50 PRINT"EXIT VALUE OF I ";I
60 END
RUN
? 1,10,1
 1  2  3  4  5  6  7  8  9  10 EXIT VALUE OF I  11

>READY
RUN
? 1,1,1 .
 1 EXIT VALUE OF I  2

>READY
RUN
? 5,1,1
 5 EXIT VALUE OF I  6

>READY
```

Figure 23 (b)

```
  10 INPUT A,B,C
* 20 FOR I=A TO B STEP C
* 30 PRINT I;
* 40 NEXT I
* 50 PRINT"EXIT VALUE OF I ";I
* 60 END
* RUN
 ? 1,10,1
 1  2  3  4  5  6  7  8  9  10 EXIT VALUE OF I  10

END AT 0060
* RUN
 ? 1,1,1
 1 EXIT VALUE OF I  1

END AT 0060
* RUN
 ? 5,1,1
EXIT VALUE OF I  5

END AT 0060
*
```

Figure 23 (c)

(6) *Interpreter errors*

These are errors discovered by BASIC at an attempt to run a program. It must be realised that when a BASIC program is typed in, each line, error-free or not, is placed in an area of RAM. These lines are scanned by BASIC and interpreted on the command RUN. Each line is inspected in line number order, and if an error is found an error message is issued giving a brief description of the error. Once BASIC finds an error the program will halt, and only when the line has been corrected can BASIC get past that line. Unless a command such as

```
RUN 7Ø
```

can be issued – RUN from line 70 – RUN will always cause execution to commence at the lowest numbered line. It is therefore very important to test each program thoroughly by making sure that every possible jump is made so that no incorrect lines are left lurking about, ready to stop the program when that unexpected piece of data is processed.

The commonest errors will usually be identified by error messages such as

UNMATCHED PARENTHESES – unequal number of left and right hand brackets.

UNDEFINED VARIABLE – a variable is used whose value has not been assigned previously. For example a line such as

```
35 LET P = Q + R – T
```

is reached but R, say, has not been assigned a value earlier in the program.

OVERFLOW – an attempt has been made to divide by zero. Check why this is so.

SUBSCRIPT OUT OF BOUNDS – an attempt has been made to use a value of a subscript larger than that allowed for in a DIM statement. Remember that if an array has not been dimensioned you are allowed 10 free elements if it has one dimension, and 10 x 10 free elements if it has two dimensions. For example, if you write

```
1Ø FOR I = 1 to 2Ø
2Ø LET A(I) = I
3Ø NEXT I
4Ø END
```

the program will run round the loop ten times, and then stop with an error message that the array subscript is out of bounds, since a reference is made to element A(11) when only A(1) to A(10) are implicitly allowed. This error can occur in certain versions of BASIC which have a CLEAR statement, even though a correct DIM statement is in the program. The following is an example of this

```
1Ø DIM A(1ØØ)
2Ø CLEAR
3Ø FOR I = 1 TO 2ØØ
4Ø LET A(I) = I
5Ø NEXT I
etc.
```

The reason for the error is that lines 10 and 20 are in the wrong order and the CLEAR should precede the DIM.

SYNTAX ERROR – the commonest error issued by BASIC, meaning that the BASIC language has been used incorrectly and this covers a multitude of errors. The commonest are those where words have been misspelt or misused. Typical of these are

```
1Ø PRIMPT X
2Ø OUTPUT X
3Ø WHEN X = 5 THEN 65
4Ø LET Y = X:P
5Ø LET P = 3(X + Y)
6O END
```

and they will all be picked up by the interpreter, and the SYNTAX ERROR message printed. The offending line can then be retyped correctly or, particularly if it is rather long, edited using a line editor, if one is available. A line editor enables one or more characters to be changed on any one line of a program.

(7) *Choosing test data*

Many programs contain errors which can be detected before it becomes too late, by the use of suitable test data. If the program copes successfully with the test data then it can fairly confidently be said that the program is safe to use for the purpose for which it is intended. For example, in section 5 of this chapter a program which tests how FOR. . .NEXT. . . loops work, is described. Three sets of test data were suggested in order to demonstrate the point. They were, respectively, where the target value of I was greater than the initial value, equal to the initial value and less than the target value. This covered all possibilities and so was good test data. If a program is written, as in activity 11, to sort a set of numbers into ascending order, then what better than a set of test data which is arranged in descending order? By choosing good test data all parts of the program are tested. There is nothing worse than having a program with a section that has never been tested and thus – as has already been mentioned – containing a possible syntax error. This problem is overcome by using a type of BASIC which is *compiled* rather than interpreted. In a compiler BASIC the whole program is analysed by a program called a *compiler* and converted into a machine code before it is run. It is this machine code program which is executed and runs much faster than an interpreted BASIC, where each line is converted into machine code more or less at run time. All the errors are detected during the compilation stage, and the final machine code program is not executed until all the errors of syntax have been corrected. A compiler will also detect an error where a GOTO instruction indicates a jump to an instruction which does not exist. However, compilers are expensive both in cost and the amount of RAM needed for them, so that not all microcomputer manufacturers offer them.

(8) *Expecting the computer to do the impossible*

There are times when a programmer can get carried away with the thrill of writing complicated programs. It is very easy to forget that a machine has only finite resources, such as a fixed amount of RAM. An example of this is the program which contains a statement such as

```
45 IF X% = 1ØØØØØØØ THEN 2ØØ
```

forgetting that a signed integer in a microcomputer has to be fitted into 2 bytes of RAM. Two bytes contain 16 bits, so that, allowing one bit for the sign, all one can hope for is a number no larger than

$$2^{15} = 32768.$$

A similar mistake is made in the program which contains

```
1Ø DIM A(2ØØ, 4ØØ)
```

thus expecting an array to be stored containing 80 000 elements, and that on a machine with only 48K of RAM.

Tail-piece

Type in and run the following short program

```
1Ø FOR I = 1 TO 2ØØ
2Ø S = S + .Ø1
3Ø NEXT I
4Ø A(1) = 1Ø
5Ø A(2) = 1ØØ
6Ø A(3) = 1ØØØ
7Ø PRINT A(S)
```

If you get the answer you expect you will be a lucky programmer.

The Operating System

Only the very simplest kind of microcomputer is without any form of backing store, that is, discs or cassettes. Any system which is as simple as this has all the programs which make it work stored in ROMs. Such programs are called *firmware* and they can only be changed by replacing one ROM with another. Anything in the way of instructions or data stored in RAM is transient, and disappears when the power is turned off. Only when cheap mass storage in the form of *bubble memories* becomes available will discs and cassettes be no longer necessary. Bubble memories have no moving parts and will eventually offer vast amounts of storage very cheaply – but they are still several years off yet.

If a computer has backing store in the form of discs, floppy or hard, then it operates under what is called an *operating system*. A magnetic disc can store a very large amount of information in the form of data or programs written in BASIC, or any other computer language, ready to be called into RAM for execution. Any set of data stored on a disc is said to be a *file*. Files on disc can be accessed very quickly because they are read by a read/write head which moves freely over the surface of the rotating disc. A magnetic disc works in very much the same way as a gramophone record in that any track can be reached by movement of the pickup arm. The difference between the two, apart from the actual way the data are stored, is that the groove on a record is a single spiral and the data on a magnetic disc are stored on a series of concentric tracks. Each track is divided into sectors so that the position of a particular file is specified by the track, and sector within that track, where the file starts.

The position and name of each file on a disc is stored within a *disc directory* which holds the names and starting locations of every file on that disc, and their length in bytes. A typical 5¼ inch disc will contain 40 concentric tracks, each of which is divided into 16 sectors. Each sector is divided into 128 bytes. This means that one such disc can contain 40 x 16 x 128 = 81920 bytes. An 8 inch diameter disc will obviously contain a lot more data than the smaller type of disc because it has a far greater area on which to record the data. An 8 inch disc can store approximately 300 000 bytes when only one side of the disc is used. If both sides are used, and the data are packed in at double the density, then the increase in capacity is considerable. Hard, as opposed to floppy, discs have a diameter of about 15 inches, and can be used to store upwards of 10 million bytes.

With the possibility of storing a very large number of files on a disc, it is essential to have these files properly organised. It is for this purpose that a disc operating system is needed, and this system in fact performs a number of functions, of which one is the handling of the files stored on a disc. The problem, or rather, one of the problems, resolved by the operating system is concerned with the storage and deletion of the files on a disc. If a file is no longer required, its name and relevant details are deleted from the disc directory, and the space it occupied is released for further use by other files. As it is very rare for two files to be of identical length, the operating system has to resolve the problem which would be caused if vast tracts of space previously occupied by deleted files were dotted all over the disc. The operating system acts as a librarian.

When a disc-based system is delivered, the operating system and the BASIC interpreter are supplied on discs and these programs are referred to as the *software*. The computer itself will be fitted with a special ROM containing a small program called a *monitor*. The monitor program will make it possible for programs to be read from the discs into RAM, or from cassettes into RAM, should cassettes be supplied. Since the operation of cassettes is very largely under the control of the person using the system, only a very elementary operating system is needed to handle them. This is because the cassettes operate in a normal audio cassette player, which has the play, rewind and record facilities under human control. All the monitor is required to do is to copy the name of the file being saved and other system information necessary on to the tape. The organisation of files on a disc, however, is far more complicated, as has already been said, which is why this is left to the operating system.

A very popular operating system in use on many microcomputers is called CP/M® and a few examples of the uses of this operating system follow.

```
A>DIR B:
B: JPFUN     BAS
B: PIP       COM
B: STAT      COM
B: DBAS9     COM
B: AWARI     BAS
B: NABEST    BAS
B: JHNUTS    BAS
B: CTS1      BAS
B: XYZPQRST  BAS
B: NORMAL    BAS
```

Figure 24

In figure 24 the system command

DIR B:

causes a list of all the files stored on the disc in drive B to be listed. The characters after the filename are called the filename *extension* and indicate whether the file contains text (.TXT) or is a BASIC program (.BAS).

CP/M is a trademark of Digital Research

The command

DIR *.BAS

will list all those files with a .BAS extension – see figure 25.

```
A>DIR *BAS
A: DEMON     BAS
A: LIZZY     BAS
A: NANDC     BAS
A: OX3D      BAS
A: AWARI     BAS
A: STARS     BAS
A: TEACH     BAS
A: HANGMAN   BAS
A: TESTER1   BAS
A: TEMPY     BAS
A: FILE1     BAS
A: GSA       BAS
A: DAMP      BAS
A: ROT       BAS
A: BOX       BAS
A: D BUG2    BAS
A: ROT2      BAS
A: BOX2      BAS
A: GRAPH     BAS
A: NORMAL    BAS
A: TEST2     BAS
```

Figure 25

The prompt

A>

shows that the main drive is drive A. If the system drive is to be drive B then the transfer of control is given by the command

A>B:

as shown in figure 26. After this command the prompt will be

```
A>B:
B>DIR
B: FPFUN     BAS
B: PIP       COM
B: STAT      COM
B: DBAS9     COM
B: AWARI     COM
B: NABEST    BAS
B: JHNUTS    BAS
B: CTS1      BAS
B: XYZPQRST  BAS
B: NORMAL    BAS
```

Figure 26

B>

and the return to drive A is made by

B>A:

The command

STAT

as shown in figure 27 will produce a summary of the amount of space available on both drives A and B. The command

STAT B:*.*

```
B>STAT
A: R/W SPACE: 104K
B: R/W SPACE: 212K
```

Figure 27

will list information about all the files on the disc at present loaded into drive B. This is shown in figure 28.

```
A>STAT B:*.*

RECS BYTS EX D:FILENAME.TYP
  19   3K  1 B:AWARI.BAS
   2   1K  1 B:CTS1.BAS
  80  10K  1 B:DBAS9.COM
   2   1K  1 B:JHNUTS.BAS
   1   1K  1 B:JPFUN.BAS
   4   1K  1 B:NABEST.BAS
   2   1K  1 B:NORMAL.BAS
  55   7K  1 B:PIP.COM
  24   3K  1 B:STAT.COM
   1   1K  1 B:XYZPQRST.BAS
BYTES REMAINING ON B:212K
```

Figure 28

The PIP command is used to copy a file, or series of files, from one peripheral to another (PIP = Peripheral Interchange Program). Discs, printers and any other devices are peripherals since they do not form part of the central processor. The command shown in figure 29 causes the file of BASIC instructions called HANGMAN, which is at present on the disc in drive A, to be copied on to the disc in drive B.

```
A>PIP
*B:=HANGMAN.BAS
*
```

Figure 29

A file can be erased from a disc by means of the ERA (ERAse) command. Figure 30 shows the command used to delete the file called HANGMAN from the current disc.

```
B>ERA HANGMAN.BAS
B>A:
```

Figure 30

```
A>DBAS9
RML 9K DISK BASIC V 3.08

>READY
```

Figure 31

Finally, in this brief introduction to an operating system figure 31 shows the operating system calling in the BASIC interpreter from disc into RAM, the interpreter being called DBAS9 in this case. As soon as the interpreter is loaded, control passes out of the hands of the operating system and into the BASIC interpreter, ready for the running of your BASIC programs.